D1414119

THE MYTH OF NATURAL ORIGINS

How Science Points to Divine Creation

THE MYTH OF NATURAL ORIGINS

How Science Points to Divine Creation

Ashby L. Camp

Ktisis Publishing
Tempe, Arizona

THE MYTH OF NATURAL ORIGINS
How Science Points to Divine Creation

by Ashby L. Camp

Copyright © 1994 Ashby L. Camp

All rights reserved. No part of this book may be reproduced or transmitted in any form or by any means without written permission from the author, except for inclusion of brief quotations in a review.

Typeset in 11/13 Palatino
by SAGEBRUSH Publications
Chandler, Arizona
Cover produced by Carlos F. Gonzalez
Phoenix, Arizona

10 9 8 7 6 5 4 3 2 1

Publisher's Cataloging in Publication Data
Camp, Ashby L.
THE MYTH OF NATURAL ORIGINS
How Science Points to Divine Creation / by Ashby L. Camp
    p. cm.
Includes bibliographical references and index
1. Evolution—Religious aspects 2. Evolution (Biology)
3. Creation 4. Life—Origin 5. Man—Origin
ISBN: 0-9642076-2-1 $9.95 Softcover
Library of Congress Number: 94-77024

Published and distributed in the United States by:

Ktisis Publishing
1413 E. Watson Dr.
Tempe, AZ 85283-3144

This book is lovingly dedicated to my daughter, Alissa, who inspired it, and to my wife, Meg, who has faithfully supported me in all my efforts to serve God. They are a blessing from the One whose grace is without limit.

WILLIAM L. CARRELL
2209 ABBOTT MARTIN RD. 12-11
NASHVILLE, TN 37215
E-Mail Theoflus@AOL.com
Ph. 615-385-5766

False ideas are the greatest obstacles to the reception of the gospel. We may preach with all the fervor of a reformer and yet succeed only in winning a straggler here and there, if we permit the whole collective thought of the nation or of the world to be controlled by ideas which, by the resistless force of logic, prevent Christianity from being regarded as anything more than a harmless delusion. Under such circumstances, what God desires us to do is to destroy the obstacle at its root.

J. Gresham Machen (1913)

TABLE OF CONTENTS

FOREWORD

The origin of the universe and all things contained therein by natural processes is widely accepted and proclaimed. The development of the first living organisms and their diversification into all the plants and animals now extant are attributed by many to natural processes. The most widely accepted explanation is usually called the theory of evolution, often taught as a law of nature based on established fact. To question its validity in the intellectual world is virtual heresy.

In *The Myth of Natural Origins*, Ashby Camp has effectively refuted these claims. The book is relatively brief but offers much more than just a superficial survey of the subject. It considers in depth the natural processes which supposedly have achieved such a supergigantic task. It is well organized, well written, and quite readable. The author has thoroughly researched the literature on the subject and has quoted extensively from authorities with outstanding credentials. Mostly these were authorities who affirm natural origins. He has weighed the evidence for natural origins very carefully, as would be expected of one with his legal training, and has arrived at the conclusion expressed in the title to his book—*The Myth of Natural Origins*.

The information in this book should go a long way toward anchoring a faith shaken by exposure to naturalistic teaching. This might very well be the faith of a young high school or college student who for the first time is encountering such teaching from someone skilled in its presentation. Anyone in a position to counsel such a person would profit from this book—minister, teacher, professional counsellor, or parent. Furthermore, it should be of interest to anyone who just wants to read an open-minded evaluation of the evidence for natural origins.

Wm. Clark Stevens
Emeritus Professor of Biology
Abilene Christian University

PREFACE

The subject of origins has been an interest of mine since I became a Christian in 1978. A few years ago, out of a desire to inoculate my daughter against the evolution propaganda flooding our society, I began collecting and organizing evidence that contradicts the notion that natural processes are an adequate explanation for our existence. The project grew to the point that I am now convinced it would benefit enough people to justify the effort and expense of publication.

Most of the scientists quoted in this book do not accept the theory of divine creation, and use of their statements is not intended to suggest otherwise. Their comments are quoted because they acknowledge data which, in my opinion, support a creationist view.

The only persons quoted (not simply cited) who, to the best of my knowledge, believe that God not only brought the cosmos into being but also supernaturally created each of the basic kinds of plants and animals are: Raymond Bohlin, Percival Davis, Robert Gange, Duane Gish, Dean Kenyon, Lane Lester, Marvin Lubenow, J. P. Moreland, Michael Pitman, and Perry Reeves. Hugh Ross and Richard Wright believe that God is the author of creation, but they seem to leave more room than the preceding group for his working through natural processes.

E. J. Ambrose, Michael Denton, William Fix, Pierre Paul Grassé, Marjorie Grene, Gertrude Himmelfarb, Sir Fred Hoyle, Phillip Johnson, G. A. Kerkut, Norman Macbeth, Jeremy Rifkin, and Chandra Wickramasinghe are best labeled as anti-evolutionists or anti-Darwinians. They deny the current scientific orthodoxy, but I am unaware of what role, if any, they assign to a supernatural Creator. The reader should assume that all others quoted endorse an essentially naturalistic concept of origins.

Nearly all of the quotes taken from secondary sources have been personally verified. Those that have not are marked with an asterisk after the author's name in the citation.

I continue to cite secondary sources for the verified quotes to give credit to those who did the initial digging. In the few instances where the secondary source has altered the punctuation or omitted a word, I have followed the primary source. I have also attempted to conform all quotes to the standards set forth in Kate L. Turabian, *A Manual for Writers*, 5th ed. (Chicago: University of Chicago Press, 1987).

On two occasions, I found that a later edition of a book cited by a secondary source also contained the relevant quote. In those cases, I give the later date and parenthetically note that the secondary source cited an earlier edition of the work.

Quotes taken from secondary sources normally do not include italics that were supplied by the secondary source. When such italics are retained, it is so indicated.

Bracketed language within a quote has been added to the original for explanation or clarification. When bracketed language appears within a quote for which a secondary source is cited, my initials indicate that I was the source of the addition.

The bibliography is annotated to provide the reader a clear idea of the quality of the works cited. That is also why the credentials of those being quoted are regularly provided in the body of the book.

The evolutionist's time scale is used throughout the book because the goal is to show that the scenario *as they have constructed it* is scientifically flawed. The use of such conventional dates is not intended as a concession to their accuracy.

Many numbers cited in the book are so large that they are expressed by the shorthand method of notation known as "powers of ten." Using this method, the number 100,000,000,000 would be expressed as 10^{11}. In other words, the superscripted number represents the number of zeroes that follow the 1.

THE MYTH OF NATURAL ORIGINS

ACKNOWLEDGMENTS

This work has been built, to a significant extent, on the research efforts of others. Many of the quotes used in the book were culled from secondary sources, as the citations make clear. Without the labor of these writers, whatever contribution I have made would not have been possible. I am indebted to them all.

As a source of relevant quotes, no book was more beneficial than W. R. Bird's excellent *The Origin of Species Revisited*. The books by Duane Gish, Marvin Lubenow, Michael Denton, and Percival Davis and Dean Kenyon not only contained useful quotes of other experts but were important primary sources. Anyone interested in pursuing this issue further should begin with these works.

The books by Hugh Ross, Robert Shapiro, William Fix, Michael Cremo and Richard Thompson, Lane Lester and Raymond Bohlin, and the book edited by Henry Margenau and Roy Varghese were also very useful. (Consult the bibliography for information on all of these books.)

I am grateful to John N. Clayton, Dr. Wayne Frair, Dr. John Mark Hicks, and Dr. George Howe for reviewing the book and permitting me to use their comments about it. A special thanks is due to Dr. Wm. Clark Stevens for taking the time to write the foreword. I appreciate his kind words.

THE MYTH OF NATURAL ORIGINS

INTRODUCTION

This book is intended to be a concise and scientifically credible critique of the naturalist's theory of origins. Its purpose is to expose the educated layman to the weaknesses and faith assumptions in the theories of cosmological, chemical, and biological evolution.

Leading scientists are quoted extensively because the thesis of the book is that the naturalistic explanation of existence is *scientifically* untenable. Each step in this explanation, from the origin of the cosmos to the evolution of mankind, is fraught with such difficulties that one wonders why it is believed, let alone dogmatically promoted. As a number of scientists have pointed out, the reasons are philosophical rather than scientific.

Those committed to a strictly materialistic view of reality are by definition closed to the influence of a supernatural being. Their philosophy demands that *everything* be explained, however implausibly, in terms of purely natural, mechanical processes. When Oxford zoologist Richard Dawkins wrote that "Darwin made it possible to be an intellectually fulfilled atheist," he exposed his own philosophical bias and that of many of his colleagues.

This bias accounts for much of the hostility exhibited toward scientists who favor divine creation. The disagreement about origins lacks the usual scientific detachment, not because one side is waging a noble fight for "true science," but because it is a clash between theistic and atheistic world views. To dispute the concept of natural origins is to challenge the atheist's creed and thus to nudge him toward a religious crisis.

How do those who deny the influence of a supernatural Creator claim that the universe, including the earth and its multitude of life forms, came into being? They say that everything "evolved" into existence, but that is not an explanation. It is simply another way of saying everything arose through a process of natural transformation. It does not describe *how* natural processes produced the cosmos (galaxies, stars, and planets) and the abundance of life we see on earth.

When one examines the particulars of this alleged evolution, it quickly becomes apparent that the theory is far weaker than we and our children have been led to believe. Indeed, it is the creation myth of modern western society.

ORIGIN OF THE COSMOS

Big Bang Theory

The dominant theory of cosmic evolution is the big bang theory. According to this theory, all the matter and energy now in the universe exploded from a super dense sort of "cosmic egg" some fifteen billion years ago. Helium and hydrogen were formed from elementary particles in the primeval fireball, and these gases later collected into huge clouds which formed galaxies. Within those forming galaxies, smaller clouds collapsed and became stars. Solar systems subsequently formed out of rotating dust clouds. *Bird*, 1:435-36.

To the extent that the term "cosmic egg" implies that matter and energy preexisted the titanic explosion, it is misleading. Einstein's theory of general relativity and certain astronomical observations lead to the conclusion that the entire universe exploded from a single point of infinite density, a mathematical point having no dimensions. In other words, all the matter and energy of the universe erupted into existence from nothing, from zero volume. *Ross*, 49; *Moreland*, 33. Moreover, the space-time theorem of general relativity developed by three British astrophysicists (Hawking, Ellis, and Penrose) demonstrated that even "space and time must have originated in the same cosmic bang that brought matter and energy into existence." *Ross* (2), 67; *Ross*, 110-11.

Problem of Ultimate Origin

One must recognize that this theory does not provide a naturalistic explanation for the origin of the universe. It simply states that the universe began with a tremendous, superhot explosion (a view for which there is a growing body of evidence); it says nothing about what caused that explosion. In other words, it begs the ultimate question. Such a beginning is perfectly consistent with an act of supernatural creation.

The cause of the big bang lies beyond the reach of science because there is no way to scientifically determine the nature of anything prior to the beginning of the universe. As noted by William Stoeger, a philosopher of science who has a Ph.D. in astrophysics from Cambridge University, "the natural sciences must always presuppose something to study and an order or regularity which characterizes the behavior of that something." *Margenau, 263.* Thus, the beginning of the universe is a boundary beyond which science cannot peek, a fact many leading scientists acknowledge.

Robert Jastrow, the founder and director of NASA's Goddard Institute for Space Studies and currently Professor of Earth Sciences at Dartmouth, makes this quite clear:

> [The] universe began in a cosmic explosion fifteen billion years ago, and the question arises as to what forces brought about that event. The reply of the cosmologist is that the circumstances of that explosion make it impossible to answer that question by scientific methods.
>
> So, one of the most important questions in the history of human thought, namely; Why do we exist?, or How did we get here?, turns out to have an answer that is beyond the reach of scientific inquiry. *Margenau, 46.*

Hugh Ross, an astrophysicist and former Post-doctoral Fellow at the California Institute of Technology, echoes the point:

> Expansion, coupled with deceleration, indicates a universe that is exploding outward from a point. In fact, through the equations of general relativity, we can trace that "explosion" backward to its origin, an instant when the entire physical universe burst forth from a single point of infinite density. That instant when the universe originated from a point of no size at all is called the *singularity*. No scientific model, no application of the laws of physics, can describe what happens before it. *Ross*, 49.

According to Stuart Bowyer, Professor of Astronomy at the University of California at Berkeley: "Ultimately, the origin of the universe is, and always will be, a mystery. Science has pressed the level of what can be explained further and further into the early universe, but the mystery is nonetheless there." *Margenau*, 32.

Arthur Schawlow, Professor of Physics at Stanford and recipient of the Nobel Prize for Physics in 1981, agrees:

> Current research in astrophysics seems to indicate that the ultimate origin of the universe may be not only unknown but unknowable. That is, if we assume the Big Bang, which present evidence strongly supports, there is no real way to find out what came before the Big Bang. *Margenau*, 106.

In the words of Louis Neel, Director of the Center for Nuclear Studies in France and recipient of the Nobel Prize for Physics in 1970:

> As a physicist, I consider physics to be an experimental science. A hypothesis is of interest only if it is possible to verify its consequences by discover-

ing new phenomena or new directions. This means that all hypotheses concerning the origin of the universe do not belong to physics but to metaphysics or to philosophy and that physicists as such are not qualified to deal with them. *Margenau, 73*.

This inability to discover the state of reality prior to the big bang has not stopped some theoretical physicists from speculating about a natural cause for the event, but such speculation should not be confused with science. A major problem with all such theories is that they must either assume a departure from the theory of general relativity, to avoid the conclusion that time itself began with the big bang, or postulate a cause that operated in a separate dimension of time. The former is difficult because the theory of general relativity has been experimentally verified. The latter is metaphysical, something repugnant to the naturalist, because the sciences know nothing of causes operating beyond the dimensional limitations of our universe. *Ross (2), 66-70, 91*.

Thus, the big bang theory does not explain the *ultimate* origin of the universe. The theory insists that matter, energy, space, and time suddenly came into existence, an event which logically requires a cause, but it is unable to identify that cause.

Biblical theism, on the other hand, explains the ultimate origin of the universe in terms of the Supreme Being, described as the greatest being imaginable. This provides a more intellectually satisfying foundation for origins because, unlike the universe, this being has always existed. He is the uncreated Creator. There is, therefore, no need to explain his existence. As philosophers Peter Kreeft and Ronald Tacelli point out, to ask who made the Supreme Being is like asking "Who made circles square?" It assumes a self-contradiction: that the uncreated Creator is a created creature. It extends the law about changing things—that every change needs a cause—beyond its limits, to the unchanging Source of change. God does not need a cause, or a maker, because he is not made or changed. He changes other things, but is not himself changed by anything. There is nothing that comes to be in him, nothing that needs a cause for its coming-into-being. *Kreeft*, 105.

Further, since this being transcends the limited spacetime dimensions of our universe, he could act independently of our time dimension. In other words, he could create before the beginning of our time. See, *Ross* (2), 69-70, 74-75. There is thus nothing at all surprising about a scientist of the stature of Henry Margenau, Emeritus Professor of Physics and Natural Philosophy at Yale, declaring that "God created the universe in an act which also brought time into existence." *Margenau*, 62.

Atheist philosophers are well aware that the big bang theory lends powerful support to the notion of a Creator. In the words of Anthony Flew, one of the best known expositors of atheism:

Notoriously, confession is good for the soul. I will therefore begin by confessing that the Stratonician atheist has to be embarrassed by the contemporary cosmological consensus. For it seems that the cosmologists are providing a scientific proof of what St. Thomas contended could not be proved philosophically; namely, that the universe had a beginning. So long as the universe can be comfortably thought of as being not only without end but also without beginning, it remains easy to urge that its brute existence, and whatever are found to be its most fundamental features, should be accepted as the explanatory ultimates.

Although I believe that it remains still correct, it certainly is neither easy nor comfortable to maintain this position in the face of the Big Bang story. *Margenau*, 241.

Problem of Heavenly Bodies

The big bang theory not only fails to provide a naturalistic explanation for the initial eruption of matter, energy, space, and time but also fails to explain how natural processes subsequently produced the galaxies, stars, and planets. According to Ben Patrusky, writing in *Science 81*:

Few cosmologists today would dispute the view that our expanding universe began with a bang—a big, hot bang—about 18 billion years ago. Paradoxically, no cosmologist could now tell you how the Big Bang—the explosion of a superhot, superdense atom—ultimately gave rise to galaxies, stars, and other cosmic lumps. *Gish* (2), 155.

As William Corliss assessed the matter in *Stars, Galaxies, and Cosmos* (1987), "Most astronomers and cosmologists freely admit that no satisfactory theory of galaxy formation has been formulated. In other words, a major feature of the universe is without explanation." *Bird*, 1:474.

Three years later, John Horgan, a senior staff writer for *Scientific American*, made the same point. He noted that one of the big questions unanswered by the big bang theory is "How and when did galaxies form?" *Horgan* (2), 111.

The problem with galaxy formation is well explained by Sir Fred Hoyle, formerly Professor of Astronomy and head of the Institute of Theoretical Astronomy at Cambridge University:

> The big bang theory holds that the universe began with a single explosion. Yet as can be seen below, an explosion merely throws matter apart, while the big bang has mysteriously produced the opposite effect—with matter clumping together in the form of galaxies. *Bird,* 1:462.

Instead of matter all the time becoming colder and more spread out, we often see it clustering together to produce the brilliant light of swirling galaxies and exploding stars. Why should this be so against expectations which appear soundly based in all other aspects of physical experience? *Bird,* 1:462.

Several years earlier, astronomer Geoffrey Burbidge of the University of California at San Diego pointed out, in the prestigious journal *Nature,* that the existence of galaxies requires very large density fluctuations within the expanding cloud of matter and radiation, but such fluctuations cannot be explained:

> [I]t is generally accepted that the existence of dense objects cannot be understood unless very large density fluctuations in a highly turbulent medium, or otherwise, are invoked in the first place. There is again no physical understanding of the situation; it is a condition which is put in, in a hypothetical state, to explain a major property of the universe. Thus these "theories" amount to nothing more than the statement that protogalaxies have a cosmological origin, and their origin cannot be understood any better than can the original baryons and leptons in an evolving universe. . . .
> . . . Probably the strongest argument against a big bang is that when we come to the universe in

total and the large number of complex condensed objects in it, the theory is able to explain so little. *Bird*, 1:462.

The origin of the solar system presents similar problems, as acknowledged by Sir Harold Jeffreys, a leading geophysicist. In his book *The Earth: Its Origin, History and Physical Constitution* (1976), he writes:

> To sum up, I think all suggested accounts of the origin of the Solar System are subject to serious objections. The conclusion in the present state of the subject would be that the system cannot exist. *Bird*, 1:417 (citing earlier edition).

A number of astronomers and physicists believe that the answer to cosmic lumpiness lies with hypothetical forms of matter (none has been detected in a laboratory experiment) called "exotic matter" or "dark matter." As explained by Hugh Ross:

> Because exotic matter only weakly interacts with radiation, it can function almost independently from radiation. Thus, exotic matter could clump while the radiation remains nearly smooth [smooth radiation is an observed fact]. Then, through the action of gravity . . . the exotic matter could attract ordinary matter to it. In this way, galaxies and galaxy clusters would form without causing huge waves in the background radiation. *Ross* (2), 30-31.

Several recent discoveries support the existence of dark matter and reveal something about its quantity in the universe (*Ross* [2], 29-42), but according to Steven Weinberg, recipient of the Nobel Prize for Physics in 1979, "the theory of galaxy formation remains obscure." *Weinberg*, 182. In fact, Marcia Bartusiak writes, "Astronomers are getting nervous. Models of galaxy formation are straining under the new data that assault them almost daily." *Bartusiak*, 317. The difficulty is evident in "the range of ideas now being considered by theorists *stumped by the mystery of galaxy formation*" (emphasis added). *Bartusiak*, 318. This is not the impression given in popular presentations of the theory.

Problem of Biotic Compatibility

Perhaps the biggest question unanswered by the big bang theory is how it produced an environment capable of sustaining any type of life. For a life-supporting environment to arise, so many things had to occur so precisely that the odds against it happening through purely natural laws are staggering. It strains credulity to attribute such miraculous fine tuning to purposeless forces.

For instance, according to Paul Davies, an internationally known professor of theoretical physics, if the expansion rate of the universe following the big bang varied more than a billionth of a billionth (10^{-18}) from what it was, life in the universe would have been impossible (because the necessary kind of star could not have formed—*Ross*, 124):

> Careful measurement puts the rate of expansion very close to a critical value at which the universe will just escape its own gravity and expand forever. A little slower and the cosmos would collapse, a little faster and the cosmic material would have long ago completely dispersed. It is interesting to ask precisely how delicately the rate of expansion has been "fine-tuned" to fall on this narrow dividing line between two catastrophes. If at time I S (by which time the pattern of expansion was already firmly established) the expansion rate had differed from its actual value by more than 10^{-18}, it would

have been sufficient to throw the delicate balance out. The explosive vigour of the universe is thus matched with almost unbelievable accuracy to its gravitating power. The big bang was not, evidently, any old bang, but an explosion of exquisitely arranged magnitude. *Bird*, 1:405-406.

The attempt to find a naturalistic cause for this incredible balance, such as Alan Guth's inflationary big bang model, simply moves the mystery one step back. If the four fundamental forces of physics were such that the big bang necessarily expanded at the rate required for a life-supporting universe (see, *Ross*, 124), why were those forces that way? Is it reasonable to believe that they just happened to be precisely what they needed to be for life to exist?

In fact, if *any* of the fundamental constants of physics or *any* of the several parameters of the universe (e.g., gravitational force, strong nuclear force, weak nuclear force, electromagnetic force, atomic ratios, mass of the universe, stability of the proton) had been only slightly different, the universe resulting from the big bang would have been incapable of supporting any imaginable form of life. *Ross*, 119-28; *Varghese*, 21-22. The significance of this fact is not lost on Robert Jastrow:

Thus, according to the physicist and the astronomer, it appears that the universe was constructed within very narrow limits, in such a way that man could dwell in it. This result is called the anthropic principle. It is the most theistic result ever to come out of science, in my view. *Varghese*, 22.

In a similar vein, Davies remarks:

It is hard to resist the impression that the present structure of the universe, apparently so sensitive to minor alterations in the numbers, has been rather carefully thought out. . . . [T]he seemingly miraculous concurrence of numerical values that nature has assigned to her fundamental constants must remain the most compelling evidence for an element of cosmic design. *Davies*, 189.

The weight of this evidence is apparent in the remarks of Edward Harrison, Professor of Astronomy at the University of Massachusetts at Amherst:

Here is the cosmological proof of the existence of God—the design argument of Paley—updated and refurbished. The fine tuning of the universe provides prima facie evidence of deistic design.

Take your choice: blind chance that requires multitudes of universes or design that requires only one. . . .

. . . Many scientists, when they admit their views, incline toward the teleological or design argument. *Ross* (2), 116.

George Greenstein, Professor of Astronomy at Amherst College, makes his inclination clear in *The Symbiotic Universe* (1988):

As we survey all the evidence, the thought insistently arises that some supernatural agency—or, rather, Agency—must be involved. Is it possible that suddenly, without intending to, we have stumbled upon scientific proof of the existence of a Supreme Being? Was it God who stepped in and so providentially crafted the universe for our benefit? *Ross* (2), 114-15.

Allan Sandage, winner of the Crafoord Prize in astronomy (equivalent to the Nobel Prize), is even less tentative: "I find it quite improbable that such order came out of chaos.

There has to be some organizing principle. God to me is a mystery but is the explanation for the miracle of existence, why there is something instead of nothing." *Ross* (2), 116.

Even with the constants of physics and parameters of the universe being what they are, the chance of a life-supporting planet arising by natural processes is extremely remote. To support life, a planet must be in the right place in the galaxy, have the right kind of star, be the right distance from the sun, have a proper mass, have a proper spin, have a proper tilt, possess a magnetic field, have the right atmosphere, etc. See, *Ross*, 128-32 for additional critical factors. According to Hugh Ross:

> About a dozen more parameters, including several atmospheric characteristics, currently are being researched for their sensitivity in the support of life. However, the twenty listed in Table 12.1 in themselves lead safely to the conclusion that much fewer than a trillionth of a trillionth of a percent of all stars will have a planet capable of sustaining advanced life. Considering that the universe contains only about a trillion galaxies, each averaging a hundred billion stars, we can see that not even one planet would be expected, by natural processes alone, to possess the necessary conditions to sustain life. *Ross*, 132.

All of this strongly suggests that natural processes are an inadequate explanation for our universe, our solar system, and our planet. It is more reasonable to believe in a "divine big bang" in which God not only exploded the cosmos into existence but also supernaturally directed the formation of the heavenly bodies.

ORIGIN OF LIFE

Spontaneous Biogenesis Theory

The work of two famous scientists, Francesco Redi (17th century) and Louis Pasteur (19th century), proved that living organisms do not arise from non-living things. *Davis*, 1-2, 41-3. This fact creates a problem for those who deny the existence or influence of a supernatural Creator because they are philosophically compelled to believe in the spontaneous generation of the first living organism. As stated by Harvard biochemist and Nobel laureate George Wald:

> We tell this story [of Pasteur's experiments] to beginning students of biology as though it represents a triumph of reason over mysticism. In fact it is very nearly the opposite. The reasonable view was to believe in spontaneous generation; the only alternative, to believe in a single, primary act of supernatural creation. There is no third position. *Wright*, 95.

Evolutionists believe that life initially arose from non-living matter in a very gradual series of stages. The typical textbook scenario suggests that lightning, ultraviolet rays from the sun, or heat from volcanoes affected gases in the primitive earth's atmosphere and changed them into more complicated organic compounds (fatty acids, amino acids, sugars, and nucleotides). These organic compounds

31

accumulated in the ocean and then linked up with each other to form very complex molecules (lipids, peptides, carbohydrates, and polynucleotides). Eventually, some of these very complex molecules combined to form the amazingly complex proteins, DNA, and RNA that are essential for life. These molecules then happened to be encased in a membrane and began functioning as the unimaginably complex living cell. *Davis*, 2, 42-3; *Wright*, 96-98; *Bird*, 1:326-27.

Problem of Geologic Evidence

A major problem with this scenario is that there is no geological evidence of a massive prelife accumulation of organic compounds in the earth's early history, despite the fact clay deposits from that time would have retained large amounts of such compounds if the hypothesized "prebiotic soup" had actually existed. *Davis*, 50; *Fix*, 192-93. As J. Brooks and G. Shaw state in their work *Origin and Development of Living Systems* (1973):

> If there ever was a primitive soup, then we would expect to find at least somewhere on this planet either massive sediments containing enormous amounts of the various nitrogenous organic compounds, amino acids, purines, pyrimidines, and the like, or alternatively in much metamorphosed sediments we should find vast amounts of nitrogenous cokes [graphite-like nitrogen-containing materials]. In fact, no such materials have been found anywhere on earth. . . . There is, in other words, pretty good negative evidence that there never was a primitive organic soup on this planet that could have lasted but for a brief moment. *Bird*, 1:336.

Problem of Complexity

Another major problem with this scenario is that it seems to be chemically impossible. Uninformed evolutionists sometimes claim that their theory of the origin of life has been experimentally proven, but that is absolutely false. In the years since 1953 when Stanley Miller and Harold Urey first produced several amino acids by applying electricity and ultraviolet light to a mixture of select gases, not a single one of the four primary construction materials for the simplest life (proteins, nucleic acids, polysaccharides, and lipids) has been produced in a laboratory. *Shapiro*, 104; see also, *Davis*, 3.

Researchers have not even succeeded in producing all of the 50 or so small organic compounds ("building blocks") from which these four primary construction materials are made. *Shapiro*, 104-5; *Davis*, 3, 47. If we cannot get this to happen with all our intelligence and technology, is it reasonable to think it happened by itself? And even if we could get it to happen by means of our intelligence and technology, would that mean that it initially happened by itself?

Facts About Experiments

Whatever significance the meager results of Miller-Urey type experiments may have had for origin-of-life study has been forfeited by the fact they were conducted under conditions that did not exist on earth at the time evolutionists claim that life was arising from non-living matter. In the first place, the experimenters eliminate oxygen from their beginning mixture of gases. If they do not, even amino acids will not form because oxygen (as little as 1 percent of the atmosphere compared to 21 percent today) acts as a poison that prevents the simpler chemicals from combining to produce more complicated forms. *Davis*, 3-4, 48.

33

Scientists are now convinced, however, that oxygen was present on the earth from its earliest ages. Oxidized (like rusting) minerals have been found in rocks dating from around the time life was supposedly arising, and calculations suggest that the effect of ultraviolet light on water vapor would have created an oxidized atmosphere. *Davis, 3-4, 48; Pitman, 138-39; Sunderland, 53-57; Wysong, 209-11; Varghese, 24-25; Bird, 1:330-32.*

Second, the experimenters begin with an atmosphere designed to optimize the synthesis of amino acids (methane and ammonia in chosen proportions), not with an atmosphere first determined to fairly represent that of the early earth. According to Christopher Chyba, a National Research Scientist at the NASA Ames Research Center, "most geochemists no longer think that Earth's early atmosphere consisted of methane and ammonia." *Chyba, 35;* see also, *Shapiro, 111-12; Wysong, 221-22; Bird, 1:332-34.*

Laboratory experiments and computer reconstructions of the atmosphere by James Walker of the University of Michigan suggest that the major component of the atmosphere was carbon dioxide and nitrogen spewed out by volcanoes. As science writer John Horgan recognizes, "Such an atmosphere would not have been conducive to the synthesis of amino acids and other precursors of life." *Horgan, 121.*

Third, the experimenters artificially protect the amino acids as soon as they are formed. The heat and electricity needed to create amino acids from the simpler chemicals also act to break apart those amino acids that have already formed. To prevent this, the amino acids that develop are promptly siphoned off. This would not happen in nature, so there could not be an adequate accumulation of amino acids. *Davis, 4, 48-9; Pitman, 140; Shapiro, 112-13; Bird, 1:365.*

In fact, D. E. Hull, a physical chemist, calculated the likely concentration of the simplest amino acid, glycine, that might have developed under the hypothesized conditions to be .2 mg. in a swimming pool full of water! Other amino acids and sugar yields would be far less. *Pitman,* 140; *Wysong,* 214-16; *Bird,* 1:340-41. As noted by Pitman:

> Hull concludes that the physical chemist, guided by proven principles of chemical thermodynamics and kinetics, cannot offer any encouragement to the biochemist who needs an ocean full of organic compounds to form even lifeless coacervates (gel-like blobs). *Pitman,* 140.

Fourth, the experimenters frequently use only short wavelength ultraviolet light, excluding the presumably more abundant long wavelength ultraviolet light, because the long wavelength light destroys amino acids after they form. *Bird,* 1:366.

Complexity of Biopolymers

The reason researchers have been unable to fabricate any of life's four primary construction materials (biopolymers) is that they are exceedingly complex. For instance, enzymes (special proteins that serve as catalysts for chemical reactions) are comprised of amino acids that must be arranged in a particular sequence. There are 20 amino acids involved in the construction of enzymes, all of which bond equally with each other. As explained by Sir Fred Hoyle and Chandra Wickramasinghe, an astrophysicist and mathematician at University College in Wales, for a typical enzyme of 200 amino acids, the odds of the amino acids naturally bonding together in the correct order may be calculated by multiplying the probability for each amino acid (1 in 20) together 200 times, or 1 in 10^{260} (*not* 10^{120} as indicated at *Shapiro,* 127).

THE MYTH OF NATURAL ORIGINS

Since an enzyme may still properly function with some variation in the order of the amino acids, Hoyle and Wickramasinghe reduce those odds to "only" 1 in 10^{20}. But since 2,000 different functioning enzymes are needed to duplicate even a bacterium, the odds against all 2,000 arising is 1 in 10^{20} multiplied together 2,000 times, or 1 in $10^{40,000}$! *Shapiro*, 127. (Note: Humans use about 200,000 types of protein in our cells—*Bird*, 1:80).

The problem facing the experimenters is actually much larger because all the amino acids they are able to produce are 50 percent L-type and 50 percent D-type (except glycine which does not have an L and D type). Since proteins in living things are made up exclusively of L-type amino acids (and glycine), the odds of getting a correct amino acid at a given place in the developing chain would, under the experimental conditions, increase from 1 in 20 to 1 in 39. *Davis*, 5, 50-51; *Wysong*, 71; *Pitman*, 140-41. The improbability of creating the entire chain would be multiplied accordingly.

To appreciate the magnitude of a number like $10^{40,000}$, one should know that there are only an estimated 10^{80} *atoms* in the known universe. *Bird*, 1:305; *Lester*, 85; *Pitman*, 252. Assuming every atom in the known universe pulsated one million times per second for five billion years, the total number of pulsations of all the atoms would be only 10^{103}! *Lester*, 85. It is no wonder that Hoyle and Wickramasinghe declare that the odds of 2,000 enzymes arising by natural processes is "an outrageously small probability that could not be faced even if the whole universe consisted of organic soup." *Hoyle*, 24.

As far as Hoyle and Wickramasinghe are concerned, the significance of such calculations for origin-of-life study is obvious:

36

ORIGIN OF LIFE

Any theory with a probability of being correct that is larger than one part in $10^{40,000}$ must be judged superior to random shuffling. The theory that life was assembled by an intelligence has, we believe, a probability vastly higher than one part in $10^{40,000}$ of being the correct explanation of the many curious facts discussed in preceding chapters. Indeed, such a theory is so obvious that one wonders why it is not widely accepted as being self-evident. The reasons are psychological rather than scientific. *Hoyle*, 130.

Many other scientists have reached similar conclusions regarding the probability of complex organic molecules arising by chance. Biochemist Harold Blum, author of a standard work on evolution, states:

But even if this [primordial] soup contained a goodly concentration of amino acids, the chances of their forming spontaneously into long chains seems remote. . . . [T]he probability of forming a polypeptide of only ten amino acid units would be something like 10^{-20}. The spontaneous formation of a polypeptide of the size of the smallest known proteins seems beyond all probability. *Bird*, 1:304.

Perry Reeves, Professor of Chemistry at Abilene Christian University, is in full agreement:

When one examines the vast number of possible structures that could result from a simple random combination of amino acid units in an evaporating primordial pond, it is mind-boggling to believe that life could have originated in this way. It is more plausible that a Great Builder with a master plan would be required for such a task. *Thomas*, 81-82.

As pointed out by E. J. Ambrose, Emeritus Professor of Cell Biology at the University of London, "To form a polypeptide chain of a protein containing one hundred amino acids represents a choice of one out of 10^{130} possibilities." *Bird*, 1:304. He cites Lovell as having acknowledged "that the probability of forming one of these polypeptide chains by chance is unimaginably small; within the boundary conditions of time and space we are considering it is effectively zero." *Bird*, 1:304.

According to Cornell astronomer Carl Sagan, this number is so large "that one could randomly assemble all the elementary particles in the universe a billion times a second for the age of the universe and never get this protein." *Sagan*, 45-46. That is why Lecompte du Nuoy, a French biophysicist formerly with the Pasteur Institute, says that the "time needed to form, on an average, one [protein] molecule in a material volume equal to that of our terrestrial globe is about 10^{243} years." *Bird*, 1:305; *Sunderland*, 130.

Hubert Yockey, an information scientist with a Ph.D. from the University of California at Berkeley, concludes:

> Clearly 10^9 years is far too short a time and the universe is far too small for the goddess to select even one molecule of cytochrome *c* [a protein— ALC] from the primitive milieu. Therefore a belief that proteins basic for life as we know it appeared spontaneously in the primitive milieu on earth is based on faith. *Bird*, 1:299.

When one moves to molecules as complex as DNA, the odds become even more astounding. In the words of Professor Ambrose:

> When we come to examine the simplest known organism capable of independent existence, the situation becomes even more fantastic. In the DNA chain of the chromosome of the bacterium *E. coli*, a favourite organism used by molecular biologists,

the [DNA] helix consists of 3-4 million base pairs. These are all arranged in a sequence that is "meaningful" in the sense that it gives rise to enzyme molecules which fit the various metabolites and products used by the cell. This unique sequence represents a choice of one out of $10^{2,000,000}$ alternative ways of arranging the bases! We are compelled to conclude that the origin of the first life was a unique event, which cannot be discussed in terms of probability. *Bird*, 1:302-03.

Frank Salisbury, Professor of Plant Physiology at Utah State University, notes in his article in *American Biology Teacher* (1971) that the DNA gene controlling the synthesis of a medium protein of about 300 amino acids would have about 1,000 nucleotides in its chain. He then explains:

Since there are four kinds of nucleotides in a DNA chain, one consisting of 1,000 links could exist in $4^{1,000}$ different forms. Using a little algebra (logarithms), we can see that $4^{1,000} = 10^{600}$. . . . [I]magine how many universes it would take to accommodate 10^{600} DNA chains! *Bird*, 1:321.

According to William Stokes in *Essentials of Earth History* (1982), this chance is so small "that it would not occur during billions of years on billions of planets, each covered by a blanket of a concentrated watery solution of the necessary amino acids." *Bird*, 1:305.

Even with absurdly optimistic assumptions, there is no way to account for the origin of a single gene consisting of only 600 nucleotides. In the words of astronomer Michael Hart:

Let us suppose (very optimistically) that in a strand of genesis DNA there are no fewer than 400 positions where any one of the four nucleotide residues will do, and at each of 100 other positions either of two different nucleotides will be equally effective, leaving only 100 positions which must be filled by exactly the right nucleotides. This appears to be an unreasonably optimistic set of assumptions; but even so, the probability that an arbitrarily chosen strand of nucleic acid could function as genesis DNA is only 1 in 10^{90}. Even in 10 billion years, the chance of forming such a strand spontaneously would be only $10^{-90} \times 10^{60}$, or 10^{-30}. *Ross (2), 141-42.*

If only 100 such genes were required to synthesize the proteins necessary for the simplest life, the odds against them spontaneously arising in ten billion years would be 10^{-3000}! *Ross* (2), 141-42. Even this, however, is too optimistic because, as Hart notes, "For them to be formed at the same time, and in close proximity, the probability is very much lower." *Ross* (2), 142.

It is thus not surprising that Hoyle concludes, "The notion that not only the biopolymers but the operating programme of a living cell could be arrived at by chance in a primordial organic soup here on the Earth is evidently nonsense of a high order." *Bird*, 1:304.

Michael Denton, a molecular biologist, is in full agreement:

> To the skeptic, the proposition that the genetic programmes of higher organisms, consisting of something close to a thousand million bits of information, equivalent to the sequence of letters in a small library of one thousand volumes, containing in encoded form countless thousands of intricate algorithms controlling, specifying and ordering the growth and development of billions and billions of cells into the form of a complex organism, were composed by a purely random process is simply an

affront to reason. But to the Darwinist, the idea is accepted without a ripple of doubt—the paradigm takes precedence! *Denton, 351.*

Such facts compel Jay Roth, Emeritus Professor of Cell and Molecular Biology at the University of Connecticut, to make the following admission:

> I have carefully studied molecular, biological, and chemical ideas of the origin of life and read all the books and papers I could find. Never have I found any explanation that was satisfactory to me. The basic problem is with the original template (be it DNA or RNA) that would have been necessary to initiate the first living system that could then undergo biological evolution. Even reduced to the barest essentials, this template must have been very complex indeed. For this template and this template alone, it appears it is reasonable at present to suggest the possibility of a creator. *Margenau, 199.*

Complexity of Living Cell

Keep in mind that we are speaking only of the probability that certain components essential for bacterial life would arise by natural processes. A collection of these organic components, however, is a long way from a living organism. As W. H. Thorpe acknowledges in *Studies in the Philosophy of Biology* (1974), "[t]he most elementary type of cell constitutes a 'mechanism' unimaginably more complex than any machine yet thought up, let alone constructed, by man." *Bird, 1:298-99.* It is that incredible complexity that prompts Richard T. Wright, Professor of Biology at Gordon College, to declare, "The transition from biopolymers to the first living cell is at present not even imaginable." *Wright, 101.*

Harold Morowitz, a Yale biophysicist, has calculated the odds of the spontaneous generation of a bacterium at 1 in $10^{100,000,000,000}$. *Shapiro, 128.* It is thus not surprising that he concluded, "Random events cannot account for the origin of life, at least not in the time available." *Schroeder*, 105. Wickramasinghe is in full agreement with that assessment: "There is not enough time, there's not enough resources and there's no way in which that could have happened on earth." *Varghese, 26.*

Chemist John Keosian, writing in *Cosmochemical Evolution and the Origins of Life* (1974), reaches a similar conclusion:

[T]he simplest heterotrophic cell is an intricate structural and metabolic unit of harmoniously co-ordinated parts and chemical pathways. Its spontaneous assembly out of the environment, granting the unlikely simultaneous presence of all the parts, is not a believable possibility. *Bird, 1:303.*

Scientific testimony as to the absurdity of the creation of life by natural processes is abundant. For instance, Gerald Schroeder, who has a Ph.D. in physics from M.I.T., states, "It is statistically improbable, in fact, essentially impossible, that random events produced [the first] life." *Schroeder, 112.*

Robert Shapiro, a chemistry professor at NYU and an expert on DNA research, states:

The improbability involved in generating even one bacterium is so large that it reduces all considerations of space and time to nothingness. Given such odds, the time until the black holes evaporate and the space to the ends of the universe would make no difference at all. If we were to wait, we would truly be waiting for a miracle. *Shapiro, 128.*

Harold Urey, a Nobel laureate and famous origin-of-life researcher, states:

> [A]ll of us who study the origin of life find that the more we look into it, the more we feel it is too complex to have evolved anywhere. We all believe as an article of faith that life evolved from dead matter on this planet. It is just that its complexity is so great, it is hard for us to imagine that it did. *Bird*, 1:325.

Chandra Wickramasinghe, astrophysicist and mathematician at University College in Wales, states:

> [I]f you investigate a living system that is before us, that is accessible to us, one is driven to the conclusion, inescapably, that living systems could not have been generated by random processes, within a finite time-scale, in a finite universe. *Varghese*, 33.

Francis Crick, recipient of the Nobel Prize for the discovery of the structure of DNA, states, "[T]he origin of life appears at the moment to be almost a miracle, so many are the conditions which would have had to have been satisfactory to get it going." *Pitman*, 148.

Harold Klein, professor at Santa Clara University and chairman of the National Academy of Sciences committee that reviewed origin-of-life research, states, "The simplest bacterium is so damn complicated from the point of a chemist that it is almost impossible to imagine how it happened." *Horgan*, 120.

Hugh Ross, astrophysicist and former Post-doctoral Fellow at the California Institute of Technology, states:

> My point is that the universe is at least ten billion orders of magnitude ($10^{10,000,000,000}$ times) too small or too young for life to have assembled itself by natu-

ral processes. Such calculations have been made by researchers, both theists and non-theists, in a variety of disciplines. *Ross, 138.*

Scientific Faith

Evolutionists believe in the spontaneous generation of the first life, in spite of these staggering improbabilities, because they have faith in some undiscovered organizing principle or process. In other words, they are convinced on philosophical grounds that some guiding principle was at work, and thus the improbability of the random organization of life is not seen as a bar to its natural genesis.

As explained by Robert Shapiro:

We have seen that self-replicating systems capable of Darwinian evolution appear too complex to have arisen suddenly from a prebiotic soup. This conclusion applies both to nucleic acid systems and to hypothetical protein-based genetic systems. Another evolutionary principle is therefore needed to take us across the gap from mixtures of simple natural chemicals to the first effective replicator. *This principle has not yet been described in detail or demonstrated, but it is anticipated, and given names such as chemical evolution and self-organization of matter.* The existence of the principle is taken for granted in the philosophy of dialectical materialism, as applied to the origin of life by Alexander Oparin. *Shapiro, 207 (emphasis added).*

The problem with such faith has been clearly pointed out by Sir Fred Hoyle:

If there were some deep principle that drove organic systems toward living systems, the operation of the principle should easily be demonstrable in a test tube in half a morning. Needless to say, no such demonstration has ever been given. Nothing happens when organic materials are subjected to the usual prescriptions of showers of electrical sparks or drenched in ultraviolet light, except the eventual production of a tarry sludge. *Shapiro*, 208.*

The current state of affairs is well summarized by Robert Gange, a research scientist with a Ph.D. in physics:

[T]he likelihood of life having occurred through a chemical accident is, for all intents and purposes, zero. This does not mean that faith in a miraculous accident will not continue. But it does mean that those who believe it do so because they are philosophically committed to the notion that all that exists is matter and its motion. In other words, they do so for reasons of philosophy and not science. *Gange, 77.*

Noted physicist and astronomer Robert Jastrow made this same point almost a decade earlier:

At present, science has no satisfactory answer to the question of the origin of life on earth.

Perhaps the appearance of life on the earth is a miracle. Scientists are reluctant to accept that view, but their choices are limited; *either* life was created on the earth by the will of a being outside the grasp of scientific understanding, *or* it evolved on our planet spontaneously, through chemical reactions occurring in nonliving matter lying on the surface of the planet.

The first theory places the question of the origin of life beyond the reach of scientific inquiry. It is a statement of faith in the power of a Supreme Being not subject to the laws of science.

The second theory is also an act of faith. The act of faith consists in assuming that the scientific [meaning naturalistic] view of the origin of life is correct, without having concrete evidence to support that belief. *Jastrow,* 62-63.

The truth of Gange's and Jastrow's assessment is clearly illustrated by the often-quoted comment of George Wald, a biochemist at Harvard:

One has only to contemplate the magnitude of this task to concede that the spontaneous generation of a living organism is impossible. Yet here we are—as a result, I believe, of spontaneous generation. *Shapiro,* 120.

Such "scientific faith" is also apparent in the recent remarks of Stanley Miller. Asked if he ever *entertains the possibility* that the origin of life was a miracle not reproducible by humans, Miller replied, "Not at all. I think we just haven't learned the right tricks yet." *Horgan,* 125.

New Theories

In view of the weakness of the standard theory for the origin of life, it is not surprising that several other theories have recently been proposed. Assessing this development, Horgan says, "Scientists are having a hard time agreeing on when, where and—most important— how life first emerged on earth." *Horgan,* 117. Unfortunately for the atheist, all of the new theories appear to be as flawed as the one they are seeking to replace. See, *Horgan,* 118-24; *Johnson* (2), 105-08; *Ross* (2), 138-39, 142-43. As Klaus Dose, Director of the Institute for Biochemistry at the Johannes Gutenberg University in Mainz, Germany, candidly admitted in *Interdisciplinary Science Reviews* (1988):

More than 30 years of experimentation on the origin of life in the fields of chemical and molecular evolution have led to a better perception of the immensity of the problem of the origin of life on Earth rather than to its solution. At present all discussions on principal theories and experiments in the field either end in a stalemate or in a confession of ignorance. *Gish (2),* 374.

Current Assessments

Thus, despite occasional brazen comments to the contrary by members of the scientific community, "For now, the origin of life remains an intriguing mystery." *Horgan,* 5 (quote from abstract of article contained in index). That is why the committee of the National Academy of Sciences that recently reviewed origin-of-life research concluded that "much more research is needed" (*Horgan,* 120) and why the November 1992 issue of *Discover* included the origin of life among the ten great *unanswered* questions of science. As Harvard-trained biologist Richard T. Wright boldly asserts:

But the fact is, the present evidence for the spontaneous origin of life is not strong enough to establish a plausible reconstruction, and it is certainly not strong enough to discourage belief in other options, such as the special creation of life by God. *Wright,* 110.

If only more scientists would be as honest and open minded as Dr. Werner Arber, Professor of Microbiology at the University of Basel and recipient of the Nobel Prize for Physiology/Medicine in 1978:

Although a biologist, I must confess that I do not understand how life came about.... I consider that life only starts at the level of a functional cell. The most primitive cell may require at least several hundred different specific biological macro-molecules. How such already quite complex structures may have come together, remains a mystery to me. The possibility of the existence of a Creator, of God, represents to me a satisfactory solution to this problem. *Margenau, 142.*

DIVERSIFICATION OF LIFE

Neo-Darwinian Theory

The theory of biological evolution maintains that *all* living organisms are descended from the first living cell. According to the theory, genes (subunits of DNA), which determine the characteristics of an organism's offspring, occasionally get altered (mutate) so as to produce offspring that are better able to compete with other members of their species for the limited resources of the environment. Because these genetically enhanced organisms have a higher likelihood of survival, they leave more offspring and, over time, displace the original population. When this occurs, the species is said to have evolved to the enhanced form. It is believed that the accumulation of a countless number of such slight changes over billions of years produced the wide variety of life on our planet today. *Wright*, 114-17.

Problem of Experimental Data

Contrary to this theory, numerous experiments have indicated that there are natural limits to the extent to which a species can be changed by the accumulation of genetic mutations. Geneticists have tried for nearly a century, by induced mutations and selective breeding, to transform the fruit fly into something other than a fruit fly, but their efforts have been a total failure. *Davis*, 11-12; *Wysong*, 273-74; *Fix*, 185-86. No new organ has been produced nor has the fruit fly been transformed into any other type of insect. *Davis*, 11-12. As Jeremy Rifkin reports in *Algeny* (1983):

> The fruit fly has long been the favorite object of mutation experiments because of its fast gestation (twelve days). X rays have been used to increase the mutation rate in the fruit fly by 15,000 percent. All in all, scientists have been able to "catalyze the fruit fly evolutionary process such that what has been seen to occur in *Drosophila* (fruit fly) is the equivalent of many millions of years of normal mutations and evolution." Even with this tremendous speedup of mutations, scientists have never been able to come up with anything other than a fruit fly. More important, what all these experiments demonstrate is that the fruit fly can vary within certain upper and lower limits but will never go beyond them. *Bird*, 1:124-25.

Geneticists Lane Lester and Raymond Bohlin summarize the situation by quoting Francis Hitching: "Fruit flies refuse to become anything but fruit flies under any circumstances yet devised." *Lester*, 89.

The same holds true for the extensive genetic experimentation done on the *E. coli* bacteria. According to Lester and Bohlin:

> The study of bacteria has been profoundly at the center of studies of mutations. This is because they reproduce rapidly, producing large populations and large numbers of mutants. They are also easily maintained and their environments are easily manipulated in the laboratory. Despite all their advantages, never has there arisen in a colony of bacteria a bacterium with a primitive nucleus. Never has a bacterium in a colony of bacteria been

observed to make a simple multicellular formation. Although hundreds of strains and varieties of *Escherichia coli* have been formed, it is still *Escherichia coli* and easily identifiable as such. *Lester*, 88.

It thus appears that mutations are unable to create the new structures required by the theory of biological evolution. In the words of E. S. Russell, a morphologist and former President of the Linnean Society:

> It would seem on the face of it that gene-mutations provide a very unpromising raw material for large scale evolution. Viable mutations are of the same order as the trivial differences between intra-specific races, and as such seem quite incapable of giving rise to the major divergences of structuro-functional organisation which characterise large scale habit and habitat specialisation and typal diversification. *Bird*, 1:86.

C. H. Waddington, a biologist at the University of Edinburgh, earlier (1958) made the same point in more picturesque speech:

> [A] new gene mutation can cause an alteration only to a character which the organism had had in previous generations. It could not produce a lobster's claw on a cat; it could only alter the cat in some way, still leaving it essentially a cat. *Fix*, 197.

That is why Pierre-Paul Grassé, the famous French zoologist, says, "No matter how numerous they may be, mutations do not produce any kind of evolution" (*Grassé*, 88) and why biologists Dean Kenyon and Percival Davis are convinced that "[t]he process that produces macroevolutionary changes must be different from any that geneticists have studied so far." *Davis*, 12. In other words, evolutionists simply have faith that further research will demonstrate a potential for unlimited change to occur, i.e., a mechanism for macroevolution. As Kenyon and Davis put it:

> The evolutionist, however, believes species have unlimited potential for change even if scientists have not been able to experimentally produce it. Evolutionary theory holds that the diversity of contemporary species arose through descent from a common ancestor. According to evolutionists, we must regard lack of experimentally induced unlimited change as a problem in need of research, not a basis to doubt evolution. *Davis*, 79.

Geneticists Lester and Bohlin are in full agreement:

> But one thing seems certain: at present, the thesis that mutations, whether great or small, are capable of producing limitless biological change is more an article of faith than fact. *Lester*, 141-2.

Error of Extrapolating From Microevolution

This is why it is illogical for evolutionists to cite examples of species' diversification (microevolution) as "proof" that distinct forms of life evolved (macroevolution). The fact a species diversifies, even to the point of no longer interbreeding with the parent stock, does not mean that such change could continue without limit (the amoeba-to-man scenario). The studies mentioned above seem to demonstrate just the opposite. The issue is not whether minor variations can be achieved but whether radically different and fully functional structures can be created.

Marjorie Grene, the well-known philosopher and historian of science at the University of California at Davis, made this point quite clearly several decades ago:

That the colour of moths or snails or the bloom on the castor bean stem are "explained" by mutation and natural selection is very likely; but how from single-celled (and for that matter from inanimate) ancestors there came to be castor beans and moths and snails, and how from these there emerged llamas and hedgehogs and lions and apes—and men—that is a question which neo-Darwinian theory simply leaves unasked. *Gish* (2), 14-15.

The unwarranted extrapolation from microevolution to macroevolution is being challenged by an increasing number of scientists. For example, biologists Saunders and Ho assert that there is "no evidence" for such extrapolation (*Bird*, 1:157), and paleontologists Eldridge and Tattersall write:

> What is wrong with the synthesis is not the core neo-Darwinian formulations of mechanics (natural selection working on variation within species to effect gradual change). What is wrong is the wholesale, uncritical—and unwarranted—*extrapolation* of these mechanisms via metaphors such as the adaptive landscape to embrace the evolution and diversification of all life. *Bird*, 1:157.

Problem of Genetic Improbability

Even on a theoretical level, it does not seem possible for mutations to account for the diversity of life on earth, at least not in the time available. According to Professor Ambrose, the minimum number of mutations necessary to produce the simplest new structure in an organism is five (*Davis*, 67-68; *Bird*, 1:88), but these five mutations must be the proper type and must affect five genes that are functionally related. *Davis*, 67-68. In other words, not just any five mutations will do. The odds against this occurring in a single organism are astronomical.

Mutations of any kind are believed to occur once in every 100,000 gene replications (though some estimate they occur far less frequently). *Davis*, 68; *Wysong*, 272. Assuming that the first single-celled organism had 10,000 genes, the same number as *E. coli* (*Wysong*, 113), one mutation would exist for every ten cells. Since only one mutation per 1,000 is non-harmful (*Davis*, 66), there would be only one non-harmful mutation in a population of 10,000 such cells. The odds that this one non-harmful mutation would affect a particular gene, however, is 1 in 10,000 (since there are 10,000 genes). Therefore, one would need a population of 100,000,000 cells before one of them would be expected to possess a non-harmful mutation of a specific gene.

The odds of a single cell possessing non-harmful mutations of five specific (functionally related) genes is the product of their separate probabilities. *Morris*, 63. In other words, the probability is 1 in 10^8 X 10^8 X 10^8 X 10^8 X 10^8, or 1 in 10^{40}. If one hundred trillion (10^{14}) bacteria were produced every second for five billion years (10^{17} seconds), the resulting population (10^{31}) would be only $1/1,000,000,000$ of what was needed!

But even this is not the whole story. These are the odds of getting just any kind of non-harmful mutations of five related genes. In order to create a new structure, however, the mutated genes must integrate or function in concert with one another. According to Professor Ambrose, the difficulties of obtaining non-harmful mutations of five related genes "fade into insignificance when we recognize that there must be a close integration of functions between the individual genes of the cluster, which must also be integrated into the development of the entire organism." *Davis*, 68.

In addition to this, the structure resulting from the cluster of the five integrated genes must, in the words of Ambrose, "give some selective advantage, or else become scattered once more within the population at large, due to interbreeding." *Bird*, 1:87. Ambrose concludes that "it seems impossible to explain [the origin of increased complexity] in terms of random mutations alone." *Bird*, 1:87.

When one considers that a structure as "simple" as the wing on a fruit fly involves 30-40 genes (*Bird*, 1:88), it is mathematically absurd to think that random genetic mutations can account for the vast diversity of life on earth. Even Julian Huxley, a staunch evolutionist who made assumptions very favorable to the theory, computed the odds against the evolution of a horse to be 1 in $10^{300,000}$. *Pitman*, 68. If only more Christians had that kind of faith!

This probability problem is not the delusion of some radical scientific fringe. As stated by William Fix:

> Whether one looks to mutations or gene flow for the source of the variations needed to fuel evolution, there is an enormous probability problem at the core of Darwinist and neo-Darwinist theory, which has been cited by hundreds of scientists and professionals. Engineers, physicists, astronomers, and biologists who have looked without prejudice at the notion of such variations producing ever more complex organisms have come to the same conclusion: The evolutionists are assuming the impossible. *Fix*, 196.

Renowned French zoologist Pierre-Paul Grassé has made no secret of his skepticism:

> What gambler would be crazy enough to play roulette with random evolution? The probability of dust carried by the wind reproducing Dürer's "Melancholia" is less infinitesimal than the probability of copy errors in the DNA molecule leading to the formation of the eye; besides, these errors had

no relationship whatsoever with the function that the eye would have to perform or was starting to perform. There is no law against daydreaming, but science must not indulge in it. *Grassé*, 104.

In 1967 a group of internationally known biologists and mathematicians met to consider whether random mutations and natural selection could qualify as the mechanism of evolutionary change. The answer of the mathematicians was "No." *Morris*, 64-65; *Sunderland*, 128-36. Participants at the symposium, all evolutionists, recognized the need for some type of mechanism to reduce the odds against evolution. In the words of Dr. Murray Eden of M.I.T.:

What I am claiming is that without some constraint on the notion of random variation, in either the properties of the organism or the sequence of the DNA, there is no particular reason to expect that we could have gotten any kind of viable form other than nonsense. *Sunderland*, 138.

Summarizing his and Hoyle's analysis of the mechanism of evolution, Wickramasinghe states:

We found that there's just no way it could happen. If you start with a simple micro-organism, no matter how it arose on the earth, primordial soup or otherwise, then if you just have that single organizational, informational unit and you said that you copied this sequentially time and time again, the question is does that accumulate enough copying errors, enough mistakes in copying, and do these accumulations of copying errors lead to the diversity of living forms that one sees on the earth. That's the general, usual formulation of the theory of evolution. . . . We looked at this quite systematically, quite carefully, in numerical terms. Checking all the numbers, rates of mutation and so on, we decided that there is no way in which that could even marginally approach the truth. *Varghese*, 28.

Thus, several decades have only confirmed the observation of Gertrude Himmelfarb in her book *Darwin and the Darwinian Revolution* (1959):

[I]t is now discovered that favorable mutations are not only small but exceedingly rare, and the fortuitous combination of favorable mutations such as would be required for the production of even a fruit fly, let alone a man, is so much rarer still that the odds against it would be expressed by a number containing as many noughts as there are letters in the average novel, "a number greater than that of all the electrons and protons in the visible universe"—an improbability as great as that a monkey provided with a typewriter would by chance peck out the works of Shakespeare. *Fix*, 196.

Problem of Absence of New Structures

Another problem with the theory of biological evolution is that we do not presently see mutations producing new structures on which natural selection can work. Certainly with all the life forms on earth there ought to be some evidence of an emerging structure, a not-yet functional structure that is on its way to becoming the next evolutionary advance for the species. As Pitman observes:

No nascent organ has ever been observed emerging, though their origin in pre-functional form is basic to evolutionary theory. Some should be visible today, occurring in organisms at various stages up to integration of a functional new system, but we don't see them: there is no sign at all of this radical kind of novelty. *Pitman*, 67-68.

Problem of Certain Processes and Structures

Still another problem with the theory is that many processes that occur in living things are simply inexplicable on the basis of a progressive, step-by-step development. Consider the intermediate stages in the development of a butterfly. The development of the caterpillar's hard casing and the dissolution of its organs while in that state could not have been passed on to offspring unless the capacity for metamorphosis was also present. The ancestral insect would never have survived the mutations that projected it into the chrysalid stage if it could not yet develop into an adult. *Pitman*, 71. Symbiotic relationships, such as that of the yucca moth and yucca plant, pose similar problems. *Bird*, 1:81-82.

Related to this is the fact that, as noted above, each structural step along the road from amoeba to man must "give some selective advantage, or else become scattered once more within the population at large, due to interbreeding." *Bird*, 1:87. It is extremely difficult to believe that this is the case. Even if a structure as amazingly complex as feathers were to arise, they would be of absolutely no benefit unless coordinate structures relating to nerves, muscles, and skeleton also arose. *Lester*, 98. The notion that feathers, for example, could play some other advantageous role until the full complement of structures necessary for flight arose seems to be an exercise in unrestrained imagination. As put by Lester and Bohlin:

> To summarize the problem, if incipient organs or structures were performing a different function in their preadapted state, why or how did the organ switch from this function to the one for which it is preadapted? And what took over the incipient organ's previous function? Was it lost or was it also mysteriously taken over by another preadapted

structure? To be sure, the problem of perfection in highly complex organs that has plagued Darwinism from the beginning has in no way been resolved. *Lester*, 99.

Problem of Distinctiveness of Life Forms

In addition to all of this, one wonders why, if evolutionary forces produced all of the variety of life on earth, there is any line that can distinctly be identified as a species. In other words, why is the world not filled with intermediate forms of every conceivable kind? Why is there not just one continuous gradation of life forms? *Davis*, 88. Instead:

> The overall picture of life on Earth today is so discontinuous, the gaps between the different types so obvious, that, as Steven Stanley reminds us in his recent book *Macroevolution*, if our knowledge of biology was restricted to those species presently existing on Earth, "we might wonder whether the doctrine of evolution would qualify as anything more than an outrageous hypothesis." *Denton*, 157-58.

Problem of Fossil Record

But perhaps the greatest problem for the theory of biological evolution is the fossil record. Even if it were theoretically possible for all present forms of life to have evolved from a common ancestor, one would still need to ask whether that is what actually occurred. That question can only be answered, from a scientific standpoint, by an examination of the historical record of life on the planet, i.e., by an examination of the fossil record. As put by Wilfred Le Gros Clark, a well known British evolutionist:

That evolution actually *did* occur can only be scientifically established by the discovery of the fossilized remains of representative samples of those intermediate types which have been postulated on the basis of the indirect evidence. In other words, the really crucial evidence for evolution must be provided by the paleontologist whose business it is to study the evidence of the fossil record. *Gish**, 27.

Systematic Gaps

If biological evolution actually occurred, for each life form in the fossil record one would expect to find a series of transitional forms gradually leading up to it. In other words, one would not expect organisms to suddenly appear in the record without any evidence of ancestral forms. That, however, is precisely what one finds.

As Harvard paleontologist Stephen Gould acknowledges, "New species almost always appeared suddenly in the fossil record with no intermediate links to ancestors in older rocks of the same region." *Bird*, 1:47. Another Harvard paleontologist, George Gaylord Simpson, made the same observation a couple of decades earlier:

> [I]t remains true, as every paleontologist knows, that *most* new species, genera, and families and that nearly all new categories above the level of families appear in the record suddenly and are not led up to by known, gradual, completely continuous transitional sequences. *Bird*, 1:47.

In the words of Derek Ager, a paleontologist at Imperial College:

> The point emerges that, if we examine the fossil record in detail whether at the level of orders or of

species, we find—over and over again—not gradual evolution, but the sudden explosion of one group at the expense of another. *Bird**, 1:55.

Over ninety-five percent of the roughly 30 known living phyla (major groups of life forms based upon large differences in form or structure, especially basic body plans) of plants and animals appear within a geologically brief period of time around the Precambrian-Cambrian boundary (570 million years ago), and none of these advanced forms of life has a fossil ancestor. *Davis*, 22, 92-95.

As Daniel Axelrod summarized the situation in an article in *Science*:

However, when we turn to examine the Precambrian rocks for the forerunners of these Early Cambrian fossils, they are nowhere to be found. Many thick (over 5,000 feet) sections of sedimentary rock are now known to lie in unbroken succession below strata containing the earliest Cambrian fossils. These sediments apparently were suitable for the preservation of fossils because they are often identical with overlying rocks which are fossiliferous, yet no fossils are found in them. *Gish*, 56.

According to biologist Richard T. Wright, things have not changed in the decades since Axelrod wrote those words:

Explanations offered for the lack of fossils prior to the Cambrian are to date not very satisfactory (for example, there was an explosion of speciation as ecological niches were created and filled; all of the ancestral forms were soft bodied and not preserved). We simply do not know how or where these well-developed invertebrates originated, and this is often a part of the story that is omitted from the texts. *Wright*, 128.

This is confirmed by Robert Wesson who, with reference to the Cambrian animals, declares: "There is no indication of ancestry; no invertebrate class is connected by intermediates with any other." *Wesson*, 44.

As Michael Denton points out, the absence of fossil ancestors for the Cambrian fauna is certainly not due to a lack of effort in trying to find them:

> As we have seen, all the main invertebrate types appear already clearly differentiated very abruptly in early Cambrian rocks. An enormous effort has been made over the past century to find missing links in these rocks which might bridge the deep divisions in the animal kingdom. Yet no links have ever been found and the relationships of the major groups are as enigmatic today as one hundred years ago. *Denton*, 186.

The older (some 700 million years ago) Ediacaran fauna, first discovered in Australia in 1947, is recognized to be "a unique and extinct experiment in the basic construction of living things" (*Gould*, 16), having no relevance to the origin of the later Cambrian forms. Even if that were not the case, the Ediacaran fauna is itself quite complex (superficially resembling jellyfish, corals, and worms) and raises the same problem as the Cambrian forms. Why are there no fossil creatures between these animals and their alleged unicellular ancestors?

The total absence of transitional forms leading up to the multitude of phyla that explode on the scene at the Cambrian boundary is very difficult to square with the theory that these phyla evolved from microorganisms. Since phyla are the most basic categories (taxa) of plant and animal life, their appearance, according to the theory, would have been preceded by a massive amount of evolutionary activity occurring within a relatively brief period of time. As biologists Kenyon and Davis observe:

> This nearly simultaneous appearance of most known phyla is more remarkable when we consider that the variation within a phylum is quite small compared to how much the phyla vary from one another. In other words, there is more morphological distance between two phyla than separates representatives within phyla themselves. This means that the origins of new phyla are evolution's greatest achievement in diversifying life forms. Yet, crowded as these achievements were into the first 5 percent of the fossil record, there is an unexpected lack of fossils bridging the evolutionary distance between the phyla to document evolutionary origins for them. Although the extremely early and isolated appearances of most phyla are certainly a dramatic feature of the fossil record, this pattern receives little attention in most biology textbooks. *Davis,* 95.

The earliest vertebrate (a type of fish) similarly appears in the fossil record without any evidence of ancestral forms, and there are no transitional forms between the groups that later appear within that subphylum, i.e., amphibian, reptile, bird, and mammal. According to Wesson:

> [T]here are no fossils leading to primitive chordates or linking them with the vertebrates to which they must have given rise. The latter showed up possessing such advances as a brain case, specialized sense organs, and calcified bones. *Wesson,* 41.

F. D. Ommanney, an evolutionist authority on fish, acknowledges this fact:

> How this earliest chordate stock evolved, what stages of development it went through to eventually

give rise to truly fishlike creatures, we do not know. Between the Cambrian when it probably originated, and the Ordovician when the first fossils of animals with really fishlike characteristics appeared, there is a gap of perhaps 100 million years which we will probably never be able to fill. *Bird*, 1:54.

Barbara Stahl, in her work *Vertebrate History: Problems in Evolution* (1985), likewise concedes that the "origin of vertebrates [is] an unsolved problem."

What remains to be understood is the early evolution of the entire ostracoderm [an order of fish—ALC] assemblage and the origin in even more ancient times of the vertebrate line from its nonvertebrate ancestral source. Difficulties of such magnitude exist, however, in the study of these matters that investigators have had to confine themselves to defining the problems and to building theories on the small amounts of evidence they do have. *Bird*, 1:214 (citing earlier edition).

According to Tracy Storer in *General Zoology* (1979):

Two major reasons for the existence of so many divergent theories on the origin of vertebrates are the significant difference in morphology between vertebrates and invertebrate phyla and the complete lack of any intermediate forms in the fossil record. *Eichman*, 55.

In fact, all the major classes of fish abruptly appear in the fossil record. Errol White, a former president of the Linnean Society and an expert on lungfishes, declares: "Whatever ideas authorities may have on the subject, the lungfishes, like every other major group of fishes that I know, have their origins firmly based in nothing." *Bird**, 1:62-63.

Alfred Romer, a Harvard paleontologist, echoes this observation:

> In sediments of late Silurian and early Devonian age, numerous fishlike vertebrates of varied types are present, and it is obvious that a long evolutionary history had taken place before that time. But of that history we are mainly ignorant. *Bird*, 1:61.

Gerald Todd, writing in *American Zoologist* (1980), expresses considerable perplexity over the sudden appearance of bony fish:

> All three subdivisions of the bony fishes appear in the fossil record at approximately the same time. They are already widely divergent morphologically, and they are heavily armored. How did they originate? What allowed them to diverge so widely? How did they all come to have heavy armor? And why is there no trace of earlier intermediate forms? *Gish*, 69.

The hypothesized fish-to-amphibian transition is likewise plagued by an absence of in-between forms. Wesson flatly states that "[t]here is no record of a transitional form between bony-finned fish and amphibians." *Wesson*, 41. Elsewhere he remarks:

> The stages by which a fish gave rise to an amphibian are unknown. There are resemblances between the first amphibians and certain (rhipidistian) fish with bony fins, but the earliest land animals appear with four good limbs, shoulder and pelvic girdles, ribs, and distinct heads. Certain bones in the fish fins correspond to bones in the tetrapod limbs, but the fin is very far from being a leg. *Wesson*, 50.

Evolutionists generally believe that the oldest known amphibian, *Ichthyostega*, evolved from an early crossopterygian fish, *Eusthenopteron*. *Davis*, 102; *Gish*, 72-3. The problem with this proposal is summarized by Kenyon and Davis:

> If crossopterygians really did evolve into amphibians, tremendous changes must have taken place. Fins must have been transformed into forelimbs. The skull had to change from two parts to a single, solid piece. The hip bones had to enlarge and become attached to the backbone. As well as changes in the skeleton, not a few changes must have occurred in organs, muscles, and other soft tissues. For example, the air bladder of the fish had to be transformed into the lungs of the amphibian.
>
> Though just a few of the many examples possible, these are enough to show how large the differences between early fish and amphibians really were. How many different transitional species were required to bridge the gap between them? And how many generations of each species must have been involved? Were hundreds or even thousands of species required? We have no way of knowing, but we do know that no such transitional species are found in the fossil record. *Davis*, 102.

That is why Colin Patterson, senior paleontologist at the British Museum, says:

> [T]he current account of tetrapod [an amphibian such as *Ichthyostega*—ALC] evolution, shown in a thousand diagrams and everywhere acknowledged as the centerpiece of historical biology, is a will-o'-the-wisp. For nowhere can one find a clear statement of how and why the Recent groups are interrelated, and the textbook stories are replete with phantoms—extinct, uncharacterizable groups giving rise to one another. *Bird*, 1:214.

Neither are there any transitional forms demonstrating the alleged evolution of amphibians to reptiles. As Wesson puts it, "The origin of reptiles is obscure, and it becomes more puzzling with the recent discovery of a small reptile dating back 338 million years, nearly as old as the oldest amphibians." *Wesson*, 41.

According to Kenyon and Davis:

It is equally difficult to find transitional forms in the fossil record between amphibians and reptiles. There is no well documented fossil sequence showing such transitions. Of course, there are many books by paleontologists describing in some detail just how this transition was to have occurred, but the fossil data is scanty. Hence, it is not surprising that there are differences of opinion among evolutionists concerning which group of amphibians gave rise to the first reptiles. *Davis*, 102, 104.

This is reflected in Ruben Stirton's comments on the subject in *Time, Life and Man* (1959): "There is no direct proof from the fossil record, but we can readily hypothesize the conditions under which it came about." *Bird*, 1:215.

The most significant alleged intermediate between amphibians and reptiles is *Seymouria*. From a purely skeletal standpoint, it could plausibly be argued as an intermediate, but there are two serious problems with that identification. First, the major difference between amphibians and reptiles is their mode of reproduction, and it appears, based on a fossil of an immature form, that *Seymouria* was wholly amphibian in its reproduction system. *Bird*, 1:215-16.

Secondly, *Seymouria* appears too late in the fossil record to qualify as an ancestor of reptiles. In the words of G. A. Kerkut, a leading biochemist who has edited a significant series of books on physiology and teaches at the University of Southhampton:

> Seymouria is sometimes thought of as a link between the Amphibia and reptiles. Unfortunately, Seymouria is found in the Permian whilst the first reptiles arose in the Pennsylvanian, some 20 or so million years earlier. Bird, 1:216.

Even at a conceptual level, experts admit that it is very difficult to imagine how the amniotic egg of the reptile could have evolved from the vastly different egg of the amphibian, especially given that reproductive viability must be maintained throughout the process. According to Denton, "The evolution of the amniotic egg is baffling." Denton, 218. The same is true of the origin of the reptilian heart:

> Trying to work out, for example, how the heart and aortic arches of an amphibian could have been gradually converted to the reptilian and mammalian condition raises absolutely horrendous problems. Denton, 219.

The alleged transformation of reptile to bird has likewise left no fossil traces. According to E. S. Russell, former President of the Linnean Society, "there are no paleontological data indicating how the transformation of reptile into bird came about." Bird, 1:282.

W. E. Swinton, an international expert on the subject, states the matter with equal clarity: "The origin of birds is largely a matter of deduction. There is no fossil evidence of the stages through which the remarkable change from reptile to bird was achieved." Bird, 1:216.

Again, even on a conceptual level, the transition from reptile to bird is hard to imagine. As described by Norman Macbeth:

To grasp how much such cases entail, consider the major components of reptile-to-bird; the development of feathers, which are very complicated objects; reform of the respiratory system; reform of the skeletal system, with the bones becoming porous, hollow, and in many cases fused; reform of the digestive system to allow increased fuel consumption while economising on weight; reform of the nervous system, especially the brain and the eyeball; construction of bills and beaks; mastery of nest building; and finally, acquisition of flight and all the homing capacities. Any one of these components would be hard to visualize, but when all have to go forward together while keeping the organisms in operation at all times, the difficulties become overwhelming. *Bird**, 1:217.

Of course, some evolutionists claim that *Archaeopteryx* is a transitional form between reptiles and birds, but this is incorrect. In the first place, each of the so-called reptilian features of *Archaeopteryx* have been known to exist in recognized species of birds (with arguable exception of the long bony tail), so there is no reason to think that *Archaeopteryx* was not simply an extinct species of bird. *Davis, 104-06; Pitman, 220-25; Sunderland, 74-75; Gish, 110-16; Morris, 101-103; Wysong, 300-01.* The fact it possessed reptilian features does not mean it was a reptile "becoming" a bird any more than a platypus's duck bill means it is a bird becoming a mammal! *Davis, 105-06; Pitman, 224.*

Gould and Eldridge agree that "curious mosaics like *Archaeopteryx* do not count." *Bird, 1:218; Pitman, 224.* Links are not links if they are mosaics of complete functional traits from other groups. What is needed to show the alleged transition is a reptile with developing (i.e., non-functional) wings, or feathers, or bird lungs, but this is precisely what is missing.

Secondly, a fossil of a more modern bird has now been found that is as old or older than *Archaeopteryx*. *Davis*, 104; *Morris*, 103; *Sunderland*, 75; *Fix*, 164; *Bird*, 1:218-19. Dr. John Ostrom of Yale, a recognized world authority on the origin of birds, commenting on this find stated (1977), "It is obvious that we must now look for the ancestors of flying birds in a period of time much older than that in which *Archaeopteryx* lived." At a conference in 1983, Dr. Ostrom stated, "It is highly improbable that Archaeopteryx is actually on the main line [to modern birds]." *Sunderland*, 75-6; *Fix*, 164; *Bird*, 1:219.

Despite bold assertions to the contrary, the fossil record similarly fails to support the hypothesized reptile-to-mammal transition. To appreciate the differing interpretations of the relevant fossils, one needs to be aware of certain skeletal differences between reptiles and mammals.

Reptiles have multiple bones in each half of the lower jaw, one of which articulates with the quadrate bone, a bone not found in mammals. Mammals, on the other hand, have a single bone in each half of the lower jaw which articulates directly with the squamosal area of the skull. In addition, reptiles have a single, rod-like bone in the ear (the columella), whereas mammals have three bones in the ear (the stapes, malleus, and incus). *Gish*, 96.

In several fossil species of the order *Therapsida*, the non-mammalian jawbones are quite small and located at the back of the jaw. The evolutionist believes that these reduced jawbones were in the process of becoming the malleus and incus of the mammalian ear and that the columella was becoming the stapes. There is, however, no fossil evidence of this transformation. "[N]ot a single fossil has ever been found which represents an intermediate stage, such as one possessing three bones in the jaw and two bones in the ear." *Gish*, 97; *Pitman*, 205. They all have either multiple jawbones and a single bone in the ear or a single jawbone and three bones in the ear.

Evolutionists claim that a few species, most notably *Morganucodon* and *Kuehneotherium*, possessed a double jaw joint, one of a reptile and one of a mammal, but the evidence of a mammalian (squamosal-dentary) jaw joint is purely circumstantial. "The evidence is extremely fragmentary and no fossils are available showing the dentary in actual contact with the squamosal of the skull." *Gish*, 98; *Pitman*, 205-06. Given that these creatures clearly possessed a powerful and fully functional reptilian (quadrate-articular) jaw joint (*Gish*, 97-98), it is difficult to believe that the muscles, nerves, and vessels necessary for a functional mammalian jaw joint were also present. More importantly, why is there no fossil evidence of the powerful reptilian jaw joint progressively weakening as it was replaced by the mammalian jaw joint?

Kenyon and Davis thus conclude:

> The fossil remains of many reptiles known as *Therapsids* have been compared with the first small, rodent-like mammals in the fossil record. While scientists have offered explanations of how the major changes leading to the features of early mammal fossils could have occurred, the fossil record does not show a progressive development of these distinguishing characteristics. *Davis*, 100.

This is consistent with the comments made decades earlier by Harvard's George Gaylord Simpson regarding the origin of all 32 orders of mammals: "The earliest and most primitive known members of every order already have the basic ordinal characters, and in no case is an approximately continuous sequence from one order to another known." *Sunderland*, 80; *Bird*, 1:63.

Roger Lewin, summarizing a scientific conference on the matter for the journal *Science* (1981), wrote: "The transition to the first mammal, which probably happened in just one or, at most, two lineages, is still an enigma." *Davis*, 100.

Of course, any transformation from a reptile to a mammal would involve far more than reconstruction of the jaw and inner ear. It would require creation of entirely new organs, systems, structures, and processes, matters about which fossils can tell us nothing. As Gish sarcastically points out:

> Furthermore, while all of the above miraculous changes were occurring [referring to changes in the jaw and inner ear], these creatures also invented (by genetic mistakes) many other marvelous new physiological and anatomical organs and processes, including a new mode of reproduction, mammary glands, temperature regulation, hair, and a new way of breathing. *Gish*, 102.

The danger of judging overall biology on purely skeletal grounds is well illustrated by the case of the coelacanth, a fish thought to have been extinct for a hundred million years until one was caught in 1938. This discovery caused great excitement because the coelacanth is a close relative of the rhipidistian fishes, those lobe finned fishes that were believed, on the basis of skeletal structure, to have given rise to amphibians. The presumption was that the coelacanth's soft biology would be transitional between that of a fish and an amphibian, but this turned out to be incorrect. According to Barbara Stahl, "the modern coelacanth shows no evidence of having . . . internal organs preadapted for use in a terrestrial environment." *Denton*, 179. Surely evolutionists would be similarly disappointed if one of their "mammal-like reptiles" became available for study.

The absence of transitional forms in the fossil record becomes even more absurd when one considers the alleged changes between certain mammals. Just consider the changes necessary for a small land mammal to evolve into a whale. *Davis*, 100-01. Consider all the changes necessary to go from the first small mammal to an elephant, a giraffe, and a bat. *Sunderland*, 83-84; *Davis*, 101-02. Yet, there is not one clear transitional form along the way! *Bird*, 1:221-22.

The claim that the recently found (and presumptuously named) *Ambulocetus natans* constitutes a transitional form between a land mammal and whales is wishful thinking on the part of evolutionists. Accepting the discoverers' reconstruction, which was done from quite fragmentary remains, this creature was about the size of a sea lion and had short, powerful front legs that were equipped with fully functional elbow, wrist, and digital joints. It also had hoofed hind legs and a long, flukeless tail! Since no pelvis was discovered, there is no way to reliably determine the animal's locomotion. *Thewissen*, 210-11. The very fact this find has been trumpeted as an intermediate link to whales is a good indication of the evolutionist's desperation regarding the fossil record.

Even the fairly modest transformation portrayed in the famous horse series in many public school texts is, in the words of Denton, "largely apocryphal." *Bird*, 1:223. The series starts with a four-toed *Eohippus*, passes through several three-toed creatures, and ends with a single-toed modern horse (*Sunderland*, 80-81), but nowhere in the world are the fossils in this series found in successive strata. When found on the same continent, like in the John Day formation in Oregon, the three-toed and one-toed are found in the same stratum. In South America, the one-toed is even found below the three-toed creature. *Eohippus* fossils have been found in surface strata alongside two types of modern horses. *Sunderland*, 81; *Wysong*, 301.

Saiff and Macbeth in part blame this horse series for the common misconception that evolutionists have discovered innumerable evolutionary paths of descent. In their words, this misconception

comes from a very deceptive picture that has been presented over and over again in the literature. This is the famous chart that shows, in seven neatly graded steps, the supposed descent of the horses from tiny *Eohippus* to the modern *Equus*. This chart is so persuasive that most readers will be shocked to learn that it is an illusion.

These seven stages do not represent ancestors and descendants. They are fossils that were taken from different times and places, and were then strung together, perhaps innocently, to show how evolution might (or should have) handled the matter. The experts, good Darwinians though they may be, do not contend that things actually occurred in this simple straightforward way. They regret that the chart was ever made and they have tried to expunge it from the record, but it persists despite their efforts and appears in one textbook after another. *Bird**, 1:223.

Denton makes an interesting point about the implications of the proposed horse series for the remainder of the fossil record:

The difference between *Eohippus* and the modern horse is relatively trivial, yet the two forms are separated by sixty million years and at least ten genera and a great number of species. The horse series therefore tends to emphasize just how vast must have been the number of genera and species if all the diverse forms of life on Earth had really evolved in the gradual way that Darwinian evolution implies. . . . If ten genera separate *Eohippus* from the modern horse then think of the uncountable myriads there must have been linking such diverse forms as land mammals and whales or molluscs and arthropods. Yet all these myriads of life forms have vanished mysteriously, without leaving so much as a trace of their existence in the fossil record. *Denton*, 186.

The absence of transitional fossil forms is by no means limited to the animal kingdom. According to Wesson, "The record of plants is even more discontinuous than that of animals." *Wesson*, 44. Particularly perplexing to evolutionary botanists is the absence of transitional forms between the two fundamental groups of plants, flowering plants (angiosperms) and non-flowering plants (gymnosperms). *Davis*, 106. According to Denton, "Like the sudden appearance of the first animal groups in the Cambrian rocks, the sudden appearance of the angiosperms is a persistent anomaly which has resisted all attempts at explanation since Darwin's time." *Denton*, 163.

Even within these fundamental groups, common descent is difficult to imagine. After confessing his faith in other evidence for the theory of evolution, botanist E. J. H. Corner of Cambridge University declares:

> but I still think that, to the unprejudiced, the fossil record of plants is in favor of special creation. . . . Can you imagine how an orchid, a duckweed, and a palm [all angiosperms—ALC] have come from the same ancestry, and have we any evidence for this assumption? The evolutionist must be prepared with an answer, but I think that most would break down before an inquisition. *Bird*, 1:234.

Speaking of the plant kingdom, Harold C. Bold, a morphologist, writes: "At this time there are no known living or fossil forms which unequivocally link any two of the proposed ancestors." *Davis**, 96.

The gaps in the fossil record are so extensive and systematic that in 1988 Harvard's Ernst Mayr wrote that there is "no clear evidence for any change of a species into a different genus or for the gradual emergence of any evolutionary novelty." *Wesson*, 40.

According to Steven Stanley, a noted paleontologist at Johns Hopkins University:

> The known fossil record fails to document a single example of phyletic [gradual] evolution accomplishing a major morphologic [structural] transition and hence offers no evidence that the gradualistic model can be valid. *Davis*, 108.

Colin Patterson, senior paleontologist at the British Museum, concurs with that assessment:

> I fully agree with your comments on the lack of direct illustration of evolutionary transitions in my book. If I knew of any, fossil or living, I would certainly have included them. . . . I will lay it on the line—there is not one such fossil for which one could make a watertight argument. *Bird**, 1:59.

David Kitts, Professor of Geology at the University of Oklahoma, puts the matter like this:

> Despite the bright promise that paleontology provides a means of "seeing" evolution, it has presented some nasty difficulties for evolutionists, the most notorious of which is the presence of "gaps" in the fossil record. Evolution requires intermediate forms between species and paleontology does not provide them. *Gish* (2), 378.

Fixity of Species

The absence of transitional forms is not the only problem the fossil record poses for Darwinism. In addition to the fact that organisms suddenly appear in the record without any evidence of ancestral forms, they also, contrary to the predictions of Darwinism, do not change over time after they appear. According to Gould:

> Most species exhibit no directional change during their tenure on earth. They appear in the fossil record looking much the same as when they disappear; morphological change is usually limited and directionless. *Bird*, 1:69.

David Raup, Curator of Geology at the Field Museum of Natural History, says:

> Instead of finding the gradual unfolding of life, what geologists of Darwin's time, and geologists of the present day actually find is a highly uneven or jerky record; that is, species appear in the sequence very suddenly, show little or no change during their existence in the record, then abruptly go out of the record. *Bird*, 1:51.

T. S. Kemp, Curator of the University Museum at Oxford, fully agrees:

> As is now well known, most fossil species appear instantaneously in the record, persist for some millions of years virtually unchanged, only to disappear abruptly .... *Bird*, 1:51.

It is with regard to the unchanging nature of fossil species, called stasis, that Eldridge, a paleontologist at the American Museum of Natural History, says:

> It is, indeed, a very curious state of affairs, I think, that paleontologists have been insisting that their

record is consistent with slow, steady, gradual evolution where I think that privately, they've known for over a hundred years that such is not the case. *Bird**, 1:146-47.

This fixity or lack of change does not apply only to extinct species. Many creatures living today have, according to the conventional timetable, remained virtually unchanged for hundreds of millions of years. Starfish have remained the same for 500 million years; some modern squid have changed little in 400 million years; cockroaches go back 250-350 million years; the horseshoe crab and the sea urchin are nearly identical to their 230-million-year-old fossil forms; the dragonfly appears to be 170 million years old; bowfin fishes have changed next to nothing in 105 million years; many frogs and toads are very similar to fossils dating back 65 million years; snapping turtles go back nearly 60 million years; a modern bat looks just like the oldest bat of 50 million years ago; alligators and porcupines have not changed appreciably in 35 million years. Many more animals could be added to the list. *Bird*, 1:65-68; *Davis*, 99; *Lester*, 106, 114; *Wysong*, 287-88; *Gish*, 61-65.

If the theory of evolution is true, why have these creatures so steadfastly resisted it? How can the incredible change required to go from amoeba to man reasonably be thought to occur through a process that reflects such tremendous stability?

The state of the fossil record, with its systematic gaps and fixity of species, prompts Mark Ridley, a zoology professor at Oxford, to declare that "no real evolutionist, whether gradualist or punctuationist, uses the fossil record as evidence in favour of the theory of evolution as opposed to special creation." *Bird*, 1:179. This is amazing when one considers that the fossil record is the only direct evidence of what actually occurred in the past.

Attempts to Explain Fossil Record

Evolutionists seek to explain the fossil data in one of several ways, none of which is adequate to save their theory.

Record Incomplete

Some claim that the fossil record is simply incomplete, that the fossils are there but have yet to be found. There are certainly more fossils to be discovered, but given that there are over 200,000,000 catalogued specimens of about 250,000 fossil species (*Bird*, 1:48), the record is no doubt adequate to uncover a good number of transitional forms if they existed in the quantities anticipated by Darwinism.

In addition, there are instances where the fossil record is perfectly continuous for periods dated at ten million years. In such a setting, it makes no sense to argue for the imperfection of the record. Professor Ambrose notes one such case in his book *The Nature and Origin of the Biological World* (1982):

> Professor Hallam of Birmingham carried out a systematic study of bivalve shell fish found in successive layers of strata formed during the Jurassic period at Lyme Regis. These deposits were laid down by a continuous process in the Jurassic seas, so there were no gaps in the record. Hallam hoped to demonstrate the operation of natural selection leading to progressive changes in individual species. He ended up with a completely contrary conclusion, that individual species appear suddenly with no intermediate forms. *Bird*, 1:108.

Systemic or Macromutations

Some have proposed that evolution does not occur incrementally but in huge leaps via systemic or macromutations (e.g., a bird hatches from a lizard's egg). This explains the absence of transitional forms because there are few if any to be fossilized. Richard Goldschmidt, a geneticist at Berkeley in the 1940's, is the name most associated with this notion. Goldschmidt appears to have been driven to this theory more by his disbelief that micromutations could ever account for the significant changes necessary for evolution to occur than by his concern over the fossil record. *Pun*, 222-24. This proposal has not been well received by the scientific community.

According to Lester and Bohlin, "The overriding consensus of geneticists and population biologists, by far, is that the feasibility of macromutations being significant in evolution is practically nil." *Lester*, 138. For instance, Stebbins and Ayala, suggest in the journal *Science* that the theory has been disproved:

The specific solution postulated by Goldschmidt, that is, the occurrence of systemic mutations, yielding hopeful monsters, can be excluded in view of current genetic knowledge. . . . *Bird*, 1:177.

Harvard biologist Ernst Mayr is more blunt in his criticism:

The occurrence of genetic monstrosities by mutation . . . is well substantiated, but they are such evident freaks that these monsters can be designated only as "hopeless". They are so utterly unbalanced that they would not have the slightest chance of escaping elimination through stabilizing selection. Giving a thrush the wings of a falcon does not make it a better flier. Indeed, having all the other equipment of a thrush, it would probably hardly be able to fly at all. . . . To believe that such a drastic mutation would produce a viable new type, capable of occupying a new adaptive zone, is equivalent to believing in miracles. *Denton*, 230.

Denton agrees with Mayr on this point:

Darwin's rejection of chance saltations [major leaps] as a route to new adaptive innovations was surely right. For the combinatorial space of all organic possibilities is bound to be so great, that the probability of a sudden macromutational event transforming some existing structure or converting *de novo* some redundant feature into a novel adaptation exhibiting, that "perfection of coadaptation" in all its component parts so obvious in systems like the feather, the eye, or the genetic code and which is necessarily ubiquitous in the design of all complex functional systems biological or artefactual, is bound to be vanishingly small. *Denton*, 319.

In addition to the speculative nature of the genetic mechanism, it seems impossible that as many "hopeful monsters" as would be necessary to explain the abundant variety of life forms could have appeared in the time available. Even if such creatures arose, what would they mate with in order to pass this quantum advancement onward? And why do we never observe any hopeful monsters being born?

Punctuated Equilibrium

Other evolutionists, most notably Gould, Eldridge, and Stanley, contend that there are gaps in the fossil record because species are rapidly created (within thousands of years) by mutations and sexual recombination occurring in small, isolated populations. These new species then stabilize for long periods of time and spread by migration. The intermediate forms are not preserved as fossils because there are so few of them and they exist for such a relatively short period of time. *Gish*, 247-49. This theory, which goes by the name of "punctuated equilibrium," is a substantial departure from the gradualism of Darwinism and is currently at the center of a debate among evolutionists about the dominant mode of evolutionary change. *Wright*, 127.

It should first be noted that this is still a reliance on the imperfection of the fossil record. It is a claim that countless intermediates existed, but they did not leave any record of their existence. At bottom, the theory is that nature accidentally produced an evolution process that proceeds in a fashion that is self-concealing. How convenient. Stanley recognizes that Darwin could not have gotten away with such a claim:

> Any claim that natural selection operated with greatest effect exactly where it was least likely to be documented—in small, localized, transitory populations—would have seemed to render Darwin's new theory untestable against special creation, and perhaps almost preposterous as a scientific proposition. *Bird*, 1:172-73.

More importantly, however, one must recognize that the theory does not explain *how* these countless small and isolated populations rapidly transformed into another species. In other words, it is simply an assertion that evolution occurred in a certain way, a theory in search of a mechanism to make it possible. As Lester and Bohlin observe:

> Technically, punctuated equilibrium is a description and not necessarily a mechanism or process. It is an attempt to describe the data of paleontology at their face value. Just what genetic mechanism is

involved in the speciation process was not initially explored. Consequently, the genetic aspects of this new development are open to a wide number of alternatives. With Neo-Darwinism, the gradual accumulation of point mutations over long periods of time was easily identified as the mechanism. No such clear-cut mechanism is available for scrutiny with punctuated equilibrium. *Lester*, 112.

The problem is that, however one slices it, "mutation remains the ultimate source of all genetic variation in any evolutionary model." *Lester*, 141. Even if one were to assume the possibility of one species rapidly evolving into another similar species, an assumption biochemist Duane Gish says "is contrary to our knowledge derived from the science of genetics" (*Gish*, 249), there is no way the massive jumps reflected in the fossil record could take place in the short periods of time proposed by the theory (and necessary to account for the absence of fossils). As Denton explains:

> Such major discontinuities simply could not, unless we are to believe in miracles, have been crossed in geologically short periods of time through one or two transitional species occupying restricted geographical areas. *Denton*, 193.

Therefore, punctuated equilibrium offers no solution for the really serious problem the fossil record poses for the theory of evolution. The serious problem is not the absence of transitional forms between species but the absence of transitional forms between the higher categories. As Denton states:

> The gaps which separated species: dog/fox, rat/mouse etc. are utterly trivial compared with, say, that between a primitive terrestrial mammal and a whale or a primitive terrestrial reptile and an

Ichthyosaur; and even these relatively major discontinuities are trivial alongside those which divide major phyla such as molluscs and arthropods. . . . To suggest that the hundreds, thousands or possibly even millions of transitional species which must have existed in the interval between vastly dissimilar types were all unsuccessful species occupying isolated areas and having very small population numbers is verging on the incredible! *Denton, 193-94.*

As for whether punctuated equilibrium can even account for the gaps existing between species, geneticist Richard Goldschmidt documented many instances in which long periods of geographical isolation failed to produce a new species. For instance, a race of the gypsy moth has been isolated on an island in North Japan for 60 million years, but in all that time, only variations below the species level have occurred. *Pun*, 223. This is consistent with Gish's view that the rapid speciation postulated by punctuationists is contrary to the principles of genetics.

Gish offers the following general assessment of the theory:

> The idea of punctuated equilibrium was invented to explain the absence of transitional forms between species, but does not even address, let alone solve, the problem of the really big gaps in the fossil record. Perhaps this is the reason that Gould, one of the architects of the punctuated equilibrium mode of evolution, still feels compelled to predict a "return of hopeful monsters." The rising popularity of the punctuated equilibrium notion of evolution is just another indication of the bankruptcy of evolution theory. *Gish*, 250.

Arguments Made in Support of Theory

The fossil record aside, evolutionists sometimes seek support for their theory in the concepts of embryological recapitulation, homology, biochemical similarities, comparative embryology, and vestigial organs, but they seek in vain. When analyzed, none of these concepts makes the case for biological evolution.

Embryological Recapitulation

Embryological recapitulation is the theory that a developing embryo, in appearance, passes through the successive stages of its species' evolutionary development. It is also called the "biogenetic law." Those subscribing to this theory allege, for example, that a human embryo has "gill slits" during its early stages of development. Only uninformed evolutionists make this argument in support of their theory because it has been totally discredited.

The so-called "gill slits" of the human embryo are neither gills (having nothing to do with respiration) nor slits (not being open into the throat). Rather they are pharyngeal pouches that develop into glands, the lower jaw, and structures of the inner ear. *Gish*, 251-52. As Langman states in *Medical Embryology* (1975), "[T]he human embryo never has gills." *Gish*, 252.

As the study of embryological development moved beyond the superficial level, it became apparent that the theory was incorrect. *Gish*, 252; *Sunderland*, 121; *Davis*, 128-33; *Wysong*, 400-01. It has long been abandoned by scientists, but unfortunately "some textbooks have not kept pace, and it is still taught." *Davis*, 132. As stated by Walter J. Bock of the Department of Biological Sciences at Columbia University, "[T]he biogenetic law has become so deeply rooted in biological thought that it cannot be weeded out in spite of its having been demonstrated to be wrong by numerous subsequent scholars." *Gish*, 251.

Ashley Montagu, a staunch evolutionist and noted anthropologist, left no doubt as to the status of this theory during a debate at Princeton University in 1980. According to Dr. Montagu:

> The theory of recapitulation was destroyed in 1921 by Professor Walter Garstang in a famous paper, since when no respectable biologist has ever used the theory of recapitulation, because it was utterly unsound, created by a Nazi-like preacher named Haeckel. *Sunderland*, 119.

Homology

Homology refers to the similarity that exists in the structures, organs, and metabolisms of different organisms. Evolutionists often cite these similarities as proof of evolution, claiming that they were passed on to the organisms possessing them by their common evolutionary ancestor. That, however, is not the only explanation available. The presence of similarities is perfectly consistent with divine creation.

A shed, a house, and a mansion are similar structures, but they did not evolve from a common ancestor. The reason they have similarities is that they were designed by intelligent beings who began with a basic concept and adapted it to different ends. Human designers seek to build on existing patterns and concepts. Thus, if an intelligent Creator designed living creatures, similarities in design are perfectly understandable. *Davis*, 32-33; *Sunderland*, 124-25. As Colin Patterson recognizes, theories of evolutionary descent "are untestable by morphology alone, which cannot discriminate descent from common ancestry, or from non-evolutionary relationship." *Bird*, 1:129.

In fact, similarities among different animals are very difficult for the evolutionist to explain because they do not follow a branching pattern as evolution would predict but show a mosaic or patchwork pattern. *Davis*, 33. Many similarities exist among organisms having no close biological relationship. This pattern is well known, as evident from the comments of zoologist D. M. Ross:

> But in general, the comparison of physiological function throughout the animal kingdom leaves one with the impression that animals of all levels possess the physiological equipment required for their particular modes of life without much reference to the phylogenetic histories of the groups to which they belong. *Bird*, 1:98.

For example, marsupials and placenta mammals are two widely different classifications, but they contain a number of creatures of almost identical skeletal structures. The evolutionist claims that a random, undirected process of mutations produced identical features in widely separated organisms. Given the tremendous odds against producing any one such set of features by chance, the odds against randomly duplicating the effort are beyond comprehension. *Davis*, 33.

The same can be said for the problem of flight. As Kenyon and Davis point out:

> The ability to fly requires a tremendously complex set of adaptations, affecting virtually every organ of the body. Yet evolutionists insist that flight has evolved independently not once but four times: in birds, in insects, in mammals (bats), and in reptiles (flying dinosaurs). *Davis*, 33.

In the words of Kenyon and Davis, it seems that similarities are like "fixed patterns or discrete blocks that can be assembled in various patterns, not unlike subroutines in a computer program." *Davis, 33.*

To use another analogy, similarities among living things are like pre-assembled units that can be plugged into a complex electronics circuit. They can be varied according to an organisms need to perform particular functions in air or water or on land. Organisms are mosaics made up from such units at each biological level. In this view, the possession of similar structures implies nothing of evolutionary descent. *Davis, 33.*

Gish makes the same point:

Is it surprising that the biochemistry (life chemistry or metabolism) of the human is very similar to that of a rat? After all, don't we eat the same food, drink the same water, and breathe the same air? *If* evolution were true, similarities in structure and metabolism would be a valuable aid in tracing evolutionary ancestries, but it is worthless as evidence *for* evolution. These types of similarities are predicted by both the creation and the evolution models. Such similarities are actually the result of the fact that creation is based upon the master plan of the Master Planner. Where similar functions were needed, the Creator used similar structures and life chemistry to perform these functions, merely modifying these structures and metabolic pathways to meet the individual requirement of each organism. *Gish, 253.*

In addition, genetic research has shown that so-called homologous structures (e.g., arm of man, wing of bird, flipper of whale) are not controlled by the same gene complexes in the different species. According to Sir Gavin de Beer, former director of the British Museum and Professor of Embryology at University College of London, in his booklet *Homology, An Unsolved Problem* (1971):

> It is now clear that the pride with which it was assumed that the inheritance of homologous structures from a common ancestor explained homology was misplaced; for such inheritance cannot be ascribed to identity of genes. . . .
>
> . . . [W]hat mechanism can it be that results in the production of homologous organs, the same "patterns", in spite of their *not* being controlled by the same genes? I asked this question in 1938, and it has not been answered. *Bird*, 1:94.

This does not square with evolution, which would predict that these similarities are the result of similar genes inherited from the common ancestor. Gish describes this as the "cruelest blow" to the homology argument and explains its impact as follows:

> If homologous structures exist because animals (or plants) which possess these similar structures have inherited them through evolution from a common ancestor which possessed the structure, then certainly these creatures should share in common the genes each inherited from the common ancestor which determined the homologous structure. In other words, the set of genes in each one of these creatures which determines the homologous structure should be nearly identical (thus "homologous"). But that is not the case. When the homologous structure is traced back to the genes which determine it, these genes are found to be completely different in the animals (or plants) possessing the homologous structure.
>
> Evolutionists believe that structures change (or evolve) because genes change (or evolve). Thus, if

genes change, certainly the structure or function governed by these genes should change. Conversely, if the structure or function has remained unchanged, then the genes governing this structure or function would remain unchanged. These are clearly the predictions that would be made if evolution were true. The actual genetic data, however, directly contradicts these predictions. *Gish*, 254.

Biochemical Similarities

A variant of the homology argument involves biochemical similarities between different organisms. The fact similarities in biochemistry (various proteins) sometimes parallel similarities in anatomy (e.g., the amino acid sequence of a certain protein in a horse is more like the sequence of that protein in a cow than in a bird) is believed by evolutionists to be confirmation of the evolutionary relationships inferred from those similarities. That the proteins of humans more closely resemble those of monkeys than those of turtles, for example, is taken as confirmation that humans share a common ancestry with monkeys. *Davis*, 34-35.

This argument, of course, in no way demonstrates evolutionary descent. Just as a common designer could be expected to employ similar structural design in his creatures, he could be expected to employ similar biochemical design. This biochemical base is adapted to the designer's different ends. *Davis*, 35.

In fact, the pattern of similarity that arises from biochemical research contradicts all expectations based on evolution. One study of cytochrome *c*, a protein involved in cell respiration, shows that two reptiles differ more from each other than a fish differs from a bird and more than a fish differs from a mammal. Another study shows a bird to differ more from other birds than from a mammal and shows a reptile to differ more from other reptiles than from birds. Closely related bacteria have been found to differ more from each other than mammals differ from either insects or amphibians. *Bird*, 1:98-99; see also, *Davis*, 35-38. Similar contradictions of Darwinian theory exist in studies of hemoglobin, myoglobin, hormones, and hereditary material. *Bird*, 1:98-99, 199-202.

Denton, a molecular biologist, concludes that such evidence actually reveals a non-evolutionary pattern:

> It is now well established that the pattern of diversity at a molecular level conforms to a highly ordered hierarchic system. Each class at a molecular level is unique, isolated and unlinked by intermediates. Thus, molecules, like fossils, have failed to provide the elusive intermediates so long sought by evolutionary biology. Again, the only relationships identified by this new technique are sisterly. At a molecular level, no organism is "ancestral" or "primitive" or "advanced" compared with its relatives. Nature seems to conform to the same non-evolutionary and intensely circumferential pattern that was long ago perceived by the great comparative anatomists of the nineteenth century.
>
> . . . There is little doubt that if this molecular evidence had been available a century ago it would have been seized upon with devastating effect by the opponents of evolution theory like Agassiz and Owen, and the idea of organic evolution might never have been accepted. *Denton*, 290-91.

Embryological Development

Closely related to the homology argument is the claim that similar embryological development in various organisms indicates common ancestry and evolutionary descent. (This is the more modern embryological argument, as opposed to embryological recapitulation.) It suffers from the same logical fallacy as the homology argument, namely that similarity means evolutionary descent. In addition, Eric Davidson of the California Institute of Technology has pointed out that "organisms indeed differ fundamentally in developmental strategy." *Bird*, 1:197. This is perhaps most obvious in the fact, noted by David Oldroyd of the University of New South Wales, that even "[a]natomically homologous parts in different related organisms appear to have quite different embryonic origins." *Bird*, 1:197.

Vestigial Organs

Evolutionists sometimes argue that modern organs that have no apparent function are vestiges (hence the term "vestigial organ") of prior evolutionary stages when they were useful. S. R. Scadding, a zoologist at the University of Guelph in Ontario, explains in *Evolutionary Theory* (1981) why this argument is invalid:

> I would suggest that the entire argument that vestigial organs provide evidence for evolution is invalid on two grounds, one practical, the other more theoretical. The practical problem is that of unambiguously identifying vestigial organs, i.e., those that have no function. The analysis of Wiedersheim's list of vestigial organs points out the difficulties. . . . Wiedersheim could list about one hundred in humans; recent authors usually list four or five. Even the current short list of vestigial structures in humans is questionable. . . .
>
> . . . Similarly, for other "vestigial organs" there is reasonable ground for supposing that they are functional albeit in a minor way. . . .

The other major objection to citing vestigial organs as evidence of evolution is a more theoretical one based on the nature of the argument. The "vestigial organ" argument uses as a premise the assertion that the organ in question has no function. There is no way, however, in which this negative assertion can be arrived at scientifically. . . .

Since it is not possible to unambiguously identify useless structures, and since the structure of the argument used is not scientifically valid, I conclude that "vestigial organs" provide no special evidence for the theory of evolution. *Bird*, 1:197-98.

As Gish points out, history shows that the more we learn about the human body, the more we realize that organs thought to be useless in fact serve a purpose:

With increasing knowledge, however, this list [of vestigial organs] has shrunk until the number has been reduced to practically zero. Important organs such as the thymus gland, the pineal gland, the tonsils, and the coccyx (tail bone) were once considered vestigial. The thymus gland and the tonsils are involved in defense against disease. The appendix contains tissue similar to that found in the tonsils and is also active in the fight against foreign invaders. The coccyx is not a useless vestige of a tail, but serves an important function as the anchor for certain pelvic muscles. Furthermore, one cannot sit comfortably following removal of the coccyx. *Gish*, 252.

Conclusion of Section

The remarks of Michael Denton place the theory of biological evolution in proper perspective and thus provide a fitting conclusion to this section:

The overriding supremacy of the myth [of Darwinian theory] has created a widespread illusion that the theory of evolution was all but proved one hundred years ago and that all subsequent biological research—paleontological, zoological and in the newer branches of genetics and molecular biology—has provided ever-increasing evidence for Darwinian ideas. Nothing could be further from the truth. The fact is that the evidence was so patchy one hundred years ago that even Darwin himself had increasing doubts as to the validity of his views, and the only aspect of his theory which has received any support over the past century is where it applies to microevolutionary phenomena. His general theory, that all life on earth had originated and evolved by a gradual successive accumulation of fortuitous mutations, is still, as it was in Darwin's time, a highly speculative hypothesis entirely without direct factual support and very far from that self-evident axiom some of its more aggressive advocates would have us believe. *Denton, 77.*

ORIGIN OF HUMANS

Bogus Nature of Standard Depiction

Most Americans have been led to believe that the fossil record documents a clear evolutionary progression from a small monkey-like creature to human beings. The depictions of this transformation in various editions of Time-Life's *Early Man* involve thirteen or fourteen steps (from *Pliopithecus* to Modern Man) in which the creature grows progressively larger, more erect, more humanly proportioned, less hairy, and less primitive in appearance. The impression is false, and the failure to correct it borders on outright dishonesty.

Not only are the first five creatures in this series (through *Ramapithecus*) contemporaries, meaning they could not have been the evolutionary ancestors of one another, but their appearance is wholly the product of an artist's imagination fueled by evolutionist assumptions. There is not adequate fossil data to permit a reconstruction of these animals, let alone to hypothesize their posture and manner of locomotion! *Clayton*, 151. *Ramapithecus*, for example, was drawn with a quasi-human physique and walking erect on the basis of a few jaw fragments and teeth. *Bird*, 1:230.

The bogus nature of this series is further revealed by the fact it contains many creatures which even evolutionists admit have no relevance for human evolution.

Ramapithecus, the most highly touted candidate for human ancestor among the first five in the series, is now generally recognized as merely the ancestor of orangutans. Even David Pilbeam of Harvard, perhaps the strongest advocate of the ancestral status of *Ramapithecus*, has declared that it must be stripped of its rank as a hominid (i.e., as being in the line of human descent). *Gish*, 140-44; *Fix*, 18-23; *Bird*, 1:230-31; *Davis*, 110.

Current Proposal

The only creatures that today are put forth as ancestors of modern humans are *Australopithecus afarensis* ("Lucy"), *Australopithecus africanus* ("Taung"), *Homo habilis*, *Homo erectus*, and archaic *Homo sapiens*, with many believing that Neanderthals are an offshoot of archaic *Homo sapiens*. The proposal that includes the most hominids begins with *Australopithecus afarensis* and promptly splits into the australopithecine branch and the hominid branch. The australopithecine branch, which includes *Australopithecus aethiopicus*, *Australopithecus robustus*, and *Australopithecus boisei*, is believed to have ended in extinction. The hominid branch progresses through *Australopithecus africanus* (many put this in the australopithecine branch), *Homo habilis*, *Homo erectus*, and archaic *Homo sapiens*, eventually becoming modern man. *Lubenow*, 51-52, 54-55; *Wright*, 145. This proposal is reflected in the chart below, adapted from *Lubenow*, 55.

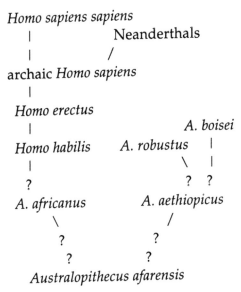

Homo sapiens sapiens
    | Neanderthals
    | /
archaic *Homo sapiens*
    |
Homo erectus
    | *A. boisei*
Homo habilis *A. robustus* |
    | \\ |
   ?   ? ?
A. africanus   *A. aethiopicus*
   \\   /
   ?   ?
   ?   ?
Australopithecus afarensis

The first point to make about this proposal is that there is no reason to include *A. afarensis* or *A. africanus* in the line of human descent. One could just as easily draw the chart with all the australopithecines forming a separate line that became extinct. In fact, Richard Leakey, a famous paleoanthropologist, actually favors that view. *Davis,* 110-12. Many others already include *A. africanus* in the australopithecine branch. *Wright,* 145; *Davis,* 110. Though this would leave *Homo habilis* without any identifiable ancestor, that is not a valid objection to the scheme. *A. afarensis* has no identifiable ancestor, nor do tens of thousands of other species that suddenly appear in the fossil record (as demonstrated above). Why assume that the evolutionary road forked at *A. afarensis* rather than at some earlier point? If history is any guide, paleoanthropologists should be very hesitant about making such assumptions.

Tarnished History of Paleoanthropology

The desire to find human ancestors is so great that the history of paleoanthropology is littered with bold pronouncements from experts that were completely wrong. Harvard's David Pilbeam, who himself was forced to withdraw his claims regarding the hominid status of *Ramapithecus*, candidly observes:

> My reservations concern not so much this book but the whole subject and methodology of paleoanthropology. . . . [P]erhaps generations of students of human evolution, including myself, have been flailing about in the dark; . . . our data base is too sparse, too slippery, for it to be able to mold our theories. Rather, the theories are more statements about us and ideology than about the past. Paleoanthropology reveals more about how humans view themselves than it does about how humans came about. *Bird*, 1:226.

The false claims regarding *Ramapithecus* are nothing compared to those made about Piltdown Man (*Eoanthropus*), a specimen found in England in 1912. For over forty years this find was hailed as one of the most important evidences of man's evolution. In 1953, after being shown in numerous exhibits and memorialized in countless textbooks, it was exposed as a hoax. The jaw belonged to an orangutan, and someone had filed the teeth and stained it to make it appear ancient. *Fix*, 12-13; *Gish* 188.

In 1922 a single molar was discovered in Nebraska, and experts soon assigned it to an apelike creature dubbed *Hesperopithecus*, or simply Nebraska Man. From that one tooth, artists provided complete drawings of this brutish "missing link." In 1927, however, it was shown that the tooth had come from an extinct pig. *Fix*, 11; *Gish* 187-88.

In 1946 an expert came into possession of some giant fossilized molar teeth which had been purchased from apothecary shops in China. He deduced from these teeth the existence of *Gigantopithecus*, an early giant apelike ancestor of man. More recent finds and reappraisal by other experts have demonstrated that this creature had nothing to do with human descent. It is seen as a giant ground-ape of the later Miocene (15-5 million years) which left no descendants. *Fix*, 24-25.

In 1959 Louis Leakey found a skull in East Africa dated to 1.75 million years. Although this skull was very similar to the previously discovered *A. robustus*, Leakey named this creature *Zinjanthropus*, or simply East African Man, and presented it as the earliest stone-tool-making man. *Fix*, 31; *Lubenow*, 157-58. Today *Zinjanthropus* is classified as *A. boisei*, with some convinced it is the same as *A. robustus*, and "there is a very broad consensus among anthropologists that both *boisei* and *robustus* were dead ends that became extinct about a million years ago." *Fix*, 32.

In 1967 a lower jaw fragment with a tooth was found in Kenya which dated at 5.5 million years. It was dubbed Lothagam Man and widely presented as the oldest hominid fossil apart from *Ramapithecus* and as one more closely resembling a human jaw than an ape jaw. In 1977 new measurements revealed that the jaw could not have belonged to an early type of man. *Fix*, 25.

As recently as 1983, a specimen touted as a "hominid collarbone" was shown to be a rib from a dolphin. *Bird*, 1:228. These errors continue to occur because there is a great deal of subjectivity in this field and because, as anthropologist Tim White observes, many anthropologists "want so much to find a hominid that any scrap of bone becomes a hominid bone." *Bird*, 1:228.

Objections to *A. afarensis*

There is certainly nothing about the appearance of *A. afarensis* to persuade one that it was related to human beings. After all, it is by definition more primitive than the other australopithecines to which it supposedly gave rise, and they are admittedly not related to humans. The very term australopithecus means "southern ape," and *A. afarensis* fits that description well.

The premier specimen of this creature ("Lucy"), currently dated to about 3.2 million years, was discovered by Donald Johanson in Ethiopia in 1974. As reconstructed (about 40 percent complete) by Johanson from widely scattered fragments, Lucy was just over three feet tall and had unusually long arms and an archaic V-shaped jaw. *Fix*, 64. Jungers, writing in *Nature*, found there was virtually no difference between the length of Lucy's upper leg bone (femur) and that of a chimpanzee of similar size and concluded that "Lucy's legs were clearly diminutive and more like those of an ape than a human" (quote from Lewin). *Bird*, 1:230, 286. According to noted paleoanthropologist Richard Leakey, Lucy's long arms are "a clue that suggests that whatever else it did, the ancient hominid was probably adept at climbing trees" (*Fix*, 64), an opinion confirmed by subsequent research (see below).

A partial skull of *A. afarensis* was reconstructed from fragments discovered in 1974 and 1975. According to Johanson, the skull "looked very much like a small female gorilla." *Cremo*, 729. Its small brain capacity (380-450 cc) overlapped that of chimpanzees (330-400 cc) and other apes. *Cremo*, 729. In the opinion of Ian Tattersall, this creature's skull is similar to the living great apes in that it has "a large chewing apparatus grafted onto the front of a relatively small braincase. Its face projects forward because of the great size of its teeth, both behind and in front of the canine." *Tattersall*, 81.

The recently found skull A.L. 444-2, which is about 75 percent complete, is even more robust. That skull, dated to around 3 million years, is described in *Science* as "[m]assive, with a projecting face and large canines." *Shreeve*, 34. Published photographs certainly confirm that description. See, *Shreeve*, 34 and *Kimbel*, 450.

A. afarensis may have possessed some degree of bipedality, but this has been seriously overplayed. Popular presentations typically ignore the fact that it was well adapted for life in the trees. Skeletal features indicate that this creature had massive shoulder and back muscles, suitable for climbing and arboreal activities. *Cremo*, 733. According to Jack Stern and Randall Susman, anatomists at SUNY at Stony Brook, the orientation of *afarensis's* shoulder joint "was an adaptation to use of the upper limb in elevated positions as would be common during climbing behavior." *Cremo*, 732. They further concluded that *afarensis* possessed "large and mechanically advantageous wrist flexors, as might be useful in an arboreal setting" (*Cremo*, 730) and "a suspensory adapted hand, surprisingly similar to hands found in the small end of the pygmy chimpanzee-common chimpanzee range." *Cremo*, 732.

M. W. Marzke agrees with this assessment of *afarensis's* hand structure. He writes in the *Journal of Human Evolution* (1983) that the curved bones of the hand "recall the bony apparatus which accommodates the well developed flexor musculature in living apes and positions it for efficient hook-like grip of the branches by the flexed fingers during arboreal climbing and feeding." *Cremo*, 732.

Brigitte Senut, a physical anthropologist at the French Museum of Natural History, studied the elbow region of Lucy's upper arm bone and found it to be "pongid-like" (pongids are apes like chimpanzees, gorillas, and orangutans). She believes that this "apelike pattern might be a result of a kind of suspension." In her view, Lucy "may be too pongid-like (i.e. specialized) to be in our ancestry." Cremo, 732.

The feet of *afarensis* were long, curved, and very muscular, similar to that of a chimpanzee. Cremo, 735. As Stern and Susman note, "There is no evidence that any extant primate has long, curved, heavily muscled hands and feet for any purpose other than to meet the demands of full or part-time arboreal life." Cremo, 736. In addition, studies by Susman indicate that this creature's big toe could be extended sideways, similar to the human thumb. Cremo, 736.

The image of *afarensis* that emerges from all this is far more apelike than one is generally led to believe. As put by Charles Oxnard, Professor of Anatomy at University of Southern California Medical School, "Pending further evidence we are left with the vision of intermediately sized animals, at home in the trees, capable of climbing, performing degrees of acrobatics and perhaps of arm suspension." Cremo, 713.

The manner of *afarensis's* bipedalism, when practiced, is a matter of debate. Oxnard and Sir Solly Zuckerman, a famous British anatomist, found significant differences between the pelvis of later (so presumably more advanced) australopithecines and that of humans. Cremo, 714-16. After extensive studies, they concluded that it was "conceivable that the habitual posture and gait of *Australopithecus* might have been unique by displaying a combination of quadrupedalism and bipedalism." Cremo, 716.

In the opinion of J. H. Prost of the University of Chicago, the australopithecines, including Lucy, were primarily quadrupedal vertical climbers. He believes that such creatures possessed the capacity for "facultative terrestrial bipedalism," meaning they could move bipedally when the situation dictated, perhaps in running from one tree to another. *Cremo*, 737-38.

According to Oxnard, the study of Lucy's knee conducted by Christine Tardieu, an anthropologist at the Museum of Natural History in Paris, revealed that "its locking mechanism was not developed." This implies "that full extension of the leg in walking, a key point in human bipedality, was lacking." *Cremo*, 734.

Stern and Susman found indications that the sacroiliac and sacrotuberous ligaments appeared to be poorly developed in *afarensis*. In their opinion, "one possible explanation [of this condition] is that the bipedal gait was like that of chimpanzees or spider monkeys." *Gish*, 162. This is reflected in their overall conclusions:

> We discovered a substantial body of evidence indicating that arboreal activities were so important to *A. afarensis* that morphologic adaptations permitting adept movement in the trees were maintained. This conclusion in and of itself, does not ineluctably lead to a second deduction that the nature of terrestrial bipedality, when it was practiced, was different from modern humans. However, we do believe this second conclusion to be reasonable even though the evidence in its favor is much less compelling than that indicating a significant degree of arboreality. *Gish*, 162.

It is sometimes asserted that the angle of Lucy's knee joint, showing a outward slant of the femur from the knee to the hip, demonstrates a human-like posture or gait, but this is not the case. Orangutans and spider monkeys have similar angles, and they both spend most of their time in trees. *Cremo*, 724, 735; *Gish*, 161-62.

In light of the preceding discussion, Gish's assessment of *A. afarensis* seems quite sound:

> Thus, while retaining the notion that "Lucy" and the other *A. afarensis* creatures walked upright, although not necessarily in a human manner, Stern and Susman maintain that these creatures were highly adapted to an arboreal, or tree-climbing, mode of locomotion. In the light of the many ape-like features of these creatures described by Stern and Susman, and in view of the conclusions of Oxnard and Zuckerman and their co-workers concerning the mode of locomotion of the australopithecines, it may be that *A. afarensis* and the other australopithecines were actually no more adapted to a bipedal mode of locomotion than are chimpanzees or gorillas, which do occasionally walk bipedally. *Gish,* 162.

Another feature of *A. afarensis* that does not get much popular press is the tremendous difference in size between the larger and smaller specimens of this species (Lucy being in the latter category). A number of experts believe that the larger specimens are actually a separate species (see, *Cremo,* 739-41), but the currently prevailing view is that the larger creatures are males. If this is correct, it suggests that *afarensis* lived in a harem arrangement rather than as bonded pairs. According to Tattersall, "In primates generally, this sex difference is associated with competition among males for females, and not with pair-bonding at all." *Tattersall,* 78. Steve Parker offers the social arrangement of modern gorillas as a possible analogy. *Parker,* 63, 66.

One needs to keep all of this in mind when exposed to the speculative and biased portrayals of *A. afarensis* that seem to abound. A personal favorite is the reconstruction of *afarensis* displayed at the American Museum of Natural

History. It shows two human-like creatures out for a stroll, the male with its arm around the full-breasted female. As curator Tattersall admits, "many details of these reconstructions are entirely conjectural. Among the attributes that can only be guessed at are hair density and distribution, skin color, form of the nose and lips, and many other features." *Tattersall*, 76. Indeed!

Objections to *A. africanus*

As for *A. africanus*, Tattersall notes that "it did not differ very conspicuously from *A. afarensis* in its build." *Tattersall*, 85. It has already been mentioned that many experts believe that this creature belongs in the australopithecine rather than the hominid branch of the proposed evolutionary tree. *Wright*, 145; *Davis*, 110. In other words, they accept that it is not relevant to the issue of human origins. The contrary view is not simply arbitrary; it is totally unreasonable given the fact that *A. africanus* is now known to have been a contemporary of *Homo erectus*. Reason, however, is no obstacle to evolutionist zealots.

Evolutionists estimate that some *A. africanus* fossils date back to three million years (*Lubenow*, 50, 171), but the oldest "reliably" dated specimens are only 1.7 million years old. *Fix*, 30-33. At the other end of the time scale, South African geologist T. C. Partridge has shown, in an unrefuted 1973 article in *Nature*, that the cave in which the premier specimen of this taxon ("Taung") was found could not be more than 870,000 years old, making the skull at most 750,000 years old. *Lubenow*, 50, 52. The general dates currently assigned to *Homo erectus* by evolutionists range from 1.8 million to 300,000 years ago. *Lubenow* 124-25. In fact, six *Homo erectus* fossil individuals have probable dates older than 1.8 million years and many such individuals are dated more recently than 300,000 years ago. *Lubenow*, 121-27.

To appreciate the significance of this overlap, it is important to recall that the theory of evolution deals with populations. Evolution occurs when a genetically enhanced form of the parent species displaces the parent population because of the increased ability of the enhanced form to compete for the limited resources available to the species. In other words, the parent population passes out of existence as the new form establishes itself. As Marvin Lubenow says, whether one speaks of Darwinism (gradual and general evolution) or punctuated equilibrium (rapid and isolated evolution):

> [I]n both models, for species A to evolve into species B, species A must precede species B in time. Furthermore, after species A has evolved into species B, any species A remnants must soon die. It is thus basic to evolution that if species B evolved from species A, that species A and species B cannot coexist for an extended length of time.
>
> The "survival of the fittest" has a flip side. It is the death of the less fit. For evolution to proceed, it is as essential that the less fit die as it is that the more fit survive. If the unfit survived indefinitely, they would continue to "infect" the fit with their less fit genes. The result is that the more fit genes would be diluted and compromised by the less fit genes, and evolution could not take place. *Lubenow*, 47.

As Phillip Johnson states it:

> Creation by natural selection and extinction by natural selection are not two separate processes but two aspects of the same process. In Darwinian terms, superior fitness means superior ability at leaving descendants. If evolution has furthered the development of capabilities like strength, vision,

and intelligence, it is only because organisms possessing these (inheritable) qualities have consistently left more descendants than have competing organisms that lack them. The more fit crowd out the less fit by definition, and there is no such thing as natural selection unless they do. *Johnson*, 104.

Thus, even if one ignores the possibility that *Homo erectus* actually precedes *A. africanus* in the fossil record, the fact these two species coexisted for more than a million years eliminates *A. africanus* as a human ancestor. The result, to quote William Fix, is that

the case for africanus as a missing link is revealed as the piece of imaginative speculation it always was. Again, we are reminded of Piltdown. The greatest difference between Piltdown and the africanus affair is that the africanus fossils are genuine. As in other cases, the deception the profession suffered with africanus was again self-inflicted through its overeagerness to read into the fossils "some special place or significance in the line of direct human descent, as opposed to that of the family of apes." *Fix*, 53.

Objections to *H. habilis*

The case for *Homo habilis* being a human ancestor is likewise built on the imagination of evolutionists. The oldest *Homo habilis* fossil is dated between 1.85 and 2.35 million years, yielding a midrange date of 2.1 million years, and the most recent *Homo habilis* fossil is dated at 1.5 million years. *Lubenow*, 129-30. The oldest *Homo erectus* fossil, the creature into which *Homo habilis* allegedly evolved, is dated at 2 million years. There are twenty-four *Homo erectus* fossil individuals (or twenty six, depending on the dating of Yuanmou Man and the Dmanisi mandible) dated between 2 million and 1.5 million years ago. *Lubenow*, 123, 130. Thus, *Homo erectus* coexisted with *Homo habilis* during the latter's entire known existence! This hardly qualifies as an evolutionary sequence.

The claim that *Homo habilis* was in the line of human descent is further shown to be absurd by Johanson's reconstruction of the species based on his 1986 discovery of some cranial and limb fragments of a *habilis* specimen (Dik-dik hill hominid dating to 1.8 million years). According to Johanson, *Homo habilis* looked just like *A. afarensis* from the neck down! It was only about three-and-one-half-feet tall and had very long arms. *Johanson*, 207-08; *Lubenow*, 164-65. Thus, not only was *Homo habilis* a contemporary of *Homo erectus*, but it was in no way a morphological transition between *A. afarensis* and *erectus*. Based on Leakey's discovery in 1984 of the skeleton of an *erectus* boy, an *erectus* adult was about six feet tall and had arms proportioned like those of modern man. *Johanson*, 207-08; *Brown*, 179-80; *Lubenow*, 136-37.

Given the morphological similarity of *habilis* and *A. afarensis*, the earlier conclusions of Oxnard and Lisowski regarding *habilis's* mode of locomotion are not surprising. Based on a study of fossil foot bones assigned to *Homo habilis*, they stated in the *American Journal of Physical Anthropology* (1980):

It is thus clear, a) that the Olduvai foot is not adapted for bipedality in the manner of man, and b) that it displays features in which it resembles the feet of arboreal creatures. Such anatomical characters as relate to bipedality in the fossil suggest usage as in an arboreal species that also walks bipedally with flattened arches (like a chimpanzee or gorilla) rather than with the high arches of man. *Gish*, 167-68.

As for *habilis's* cranial features, Brace says that the jaw and teeth of specimen OH 7 "are completely indistinguishable from a typical specimen of *A. africanus*." *Godfrey*, 258. Though the range of cranial capacity in the *habilis* specimens (about 500-800cc) is larger than the normal range for *A. africanus* (about 430-530cc), the shape of the skull and face is, according to several experts, essentially australopithecine. *Godfrey*, 258-60; *Gish*, 164-70, 173; *Fix*, 135, 141-46. Given what is now known about the body size of *Homo habilis*, it is quite possible that the larger skulls assigned to this taxon (KNM-ER 1470 and 1590) actually belonged to a separate and larger species of australopithecine about which little is known.

Lubenow rejects the characterization of Skulls 1470 and 1590 as essentially australopithecine. The size, shape, and cranial wall thickness of 1470 (1590 is more fragmentary), which Leakey himself originally described as remarkably reminiscent of modern man, convince him that they are *Homo sapien* skulls which have been incorrectly placed in the *habilis* category. *Lubenow*, 162-65. (Interestingly, some very human-looking leg bones were found in a deposit near where Skull 1470 was discovered. *Lubenow*, 161, 165; *Fix*, 145.) With a cranial capacity of about 800cc (*Fix*, 135), they fit within the lower range of modern humans. *Lubenow*, 83, 138.

Lubenow explains the australopithecine slant of the face of 1470 in terms of the evolutionary bias of those who did the reconstruction. As those involved have acknowledged, the fossil could just as easily have been given a short face. *Lubenow*, 163. Thus, as he sees it, KNM-ER 1470 and 1590 did indeed belong to a species other than *Homo habilis*, but that species was man, not another australopithecine.

Objections to archaic *H. sapiens*

The claim that *Homo erectus* evolved into archaic *Homo sapiens* is deceptive on two counts. First, it suggests that archaic *Homo sapiens* possess identifiable features that are transitional between the features of *Homo erectus* and modern *Homo sapiens* or between the features of *erectus* and Neanderthal. In fact, this group is composed of a mixed assortment of fossils which, because of their variety, cannot be said to demonstrate change toward any particular form. As Richard Klein confesses, "Morphologically, the fossils involved are too variable, even within restricted geographic regions, for summary description." *Lubenow,* 81. In the words of Ian Tattersall:

> The hominid fossil record of the past 300-400 kyr [thousand years—ALC] offers a remarkable degree of morphological variety. Yet (late-persisting *Homo erectus* aside), conventional wisdom assigns all these fossils to *Homo sapiens*, albeit of "archaic" varieties. *Lubenow,* 81.

More importantly, however, *Homo erectus* and archaic *Homo sapiens* lived as contemporaries for hundreds of thousands of years, for virtually the entire known existence of archaic *Homo sapiens*. Specimens labeled archaic *Homo sapiens* date from 700,000 all the way down to 5,000 years ago. *Lubenow,* 78-81. Evolutionists concede that *erectus* lived as late as 250,000 or 300,000 years ago (*Lubenow,* 124; *Brown,* 183), thereby admitting an overlap with archaic *Homo sapiens* of over 400,000 years, but fossils of *erectus* morphology extend well into the first millennium, even if one ignores the very recent Australian fossils. *Lubenow,* 120-27. Clearly, the notion that *erectus* and archaic *Homo sapiens* constitute an evolutionary sequence is false.

Objections to Neanderthal

The same problem confronts any attempt to construct an evolutionary sequence involving Neanderthal, a group many evolutionists now see as an isolated side branch on the human family tree. The fossil record of Neanderthal extends from about 200,000 down to 34,000 years ago. *Lubenow*, 65. Throughout this entire period of time, there existed a population with more modern features than Neanderthal and a population with less modern features. *Lubenow*, 65-68. Rather than evolution, this coexistence suggests that all of these specimens were variants within a single species, members of a race or type of *Homo sapiens*.

Erectus as *H. sapien*

Regarding the appearance of *Homo erectus*, he certainly had pronounced brow ridges and a more sloping forehead than modern man, but evolutionists have tended to exaggerate the differences. *Erectus* was not so different from modern humans as to warrant a separate species designation. Indeed, there are vast morphological differences between groups of people living today. William Laughlin of the University of Connecticut studied Eskimos and the Aleuts and, in the process, noted many similarities between those groups and the Asian *Homo erectus* people. He concluded his study with the following:

> [W]hen we find that significant differences have developed, over a short time span, between closely related and contiguous peoples, as in Alaska and Greenland, and when we consider the vast differences that exist between remote groups such as Eskimos and Bushmen, who are known to belong within the single species of *Homo sapiens*, it seems justifiable to conclude that *Sinanthropus* [an *erectus*

specimen—ALC] belongs within this same diverse species. *Lubenow, 136.*

Several experts, including Milford Wolpoff of the University of Michigan, have admitted that, given the morphological diversity of specimens qualifying as *Homo sapiens*, the distinction between *Homo erectus* and *Homo sapiens* is arbitrary:

> In our view, there are two alternatives. We should either admit that the *Homo erectus/Homo sapiens* boundary is arbitrary and use nonmorphological (i.e., temporal) criteria for determining it, or *Homo erectus* should be sunk [into *Homo sapiens*]. *Lubenow, 136.*

The similarities between *erectus* and modern man are pointed out in the Time-Life book by Edmund White and Dale Brown entitled *The First Men.* Regarding the body features of *Homo erectus*, they write:

> His bones were heavier and thicker than a modern man's, and bigger bones required thicker muscles to move them. These skeletal differences, however, were not particularly noticeable. "Below the neck," one expert has noted, "the differences between *Homo erectus* and today's man could only be detected by an experienced anatomist." *Lubenow, 136.*

This conclusion can only be bolstered by the 1984 discovery of the nearly complete skeleton of an *erectus* boy. As previously mentioned, this specimen suggests that an *erectus* adult was as tall as modern humans. Alan Walker, one of the leaders of the team that found this specimen, is quoted as saying that he doubts that the average pathologist could tell the difference between the fossil skeleton and that of a modern human. *Gish, 201.*

As for *erectus's* cranial features, the impression that he was very apelike in appearance has been created by imaginative artistic portrayals. Boyce Rensberger, a senior editor of *Science 81*, well illustrates the subjectivity of such depictions:

> Artists have also been rehabilitating Homo erectus, a hominid that lived between Australopithecus and Neanderthal, even without much change in the scientific opinion of this older species' appearance. Again, Burian is a case in point. His 1952 version shows black, apelike creatures barely distinguishable from chimpanzees. In a 1965 painting, his Homo erectus is lighter skinned and, although still hairy, more modern in aspect. Burian's 1975 Homo erectus is hairless and almost indistinguishable from people living today. *Bird*, 1:227.

The truth is that *erectus* would appear somewhat odd in his facial features, but he certainly would not strike one as anything other than human. The familiar model of *Sinanthropus* (reproduced at *Gish*, 186) should convince the most ardent skeptic of that fact. This is confirmed by the experience of Richard Leakey during the filming of a BBC series on human evolution. According to Leakey, actors who were painstakingly made up to look like *Homo erectus* were rarely noticed by the public when they were wearing modern clothes. As reported by Michael Brown:

> "When we were making the film, we took some face masks and we modeled them onto actors' faces with silicon rubber and you could not tell that they were masks," recalls Richard. "But anatomically they were correct for *erectus* in that we lost the forehead, we built up the browridges, and we gave them a prognathic [projecting face] profile. These masks took several hours to put on each morning,

and whilst waiting for the sun to appear, these actors would be standing around in clothes smoking and talking, and crowds would come by but most onlookers were unaware. It was only when someone suddenly started *looking* that it was appreciated. In a subway, chances are they wouldn't be noticed." *Brown*, 184.

This is not surprising given that anthropologists have long quipped that a clean shaven and well dressed Neanderthal would fit in with a group of modern people. *Fix*, 93-94; *Gish*, 204. Other than size, the skull of *Homo erectus* is quite similar to that of Neanderthal. *Lubenow*, 138-39. In fact, Alan Walker reports that when he put the mandible onto the *erectus* boy skull that he and Leakey discovered in 1984, they "both laughed because it looked so much like a Neanderthal." *Gish*, 201.

The fact *Homo erectus* had a cranial capacity of about 700cc (Java Modjokerto infant) to 1200cc does not mean it was intellectually primitive. This capacity puts it within the lower limits of the range exhibited in modern humans (*Lubenow*, 138), and as Lubenow notes, the variation in human brain sizes exists "with no differences in ability or intelligence." *Lubenow*, 83. The crucial element in intelligence is not brain size but brain organization. Thus, a general upward trend in skull size does not demonstrate a transition from animal to human.

Further evidence of the humanity of *Homo erectus* is provided by the things found in association with him. According to Lubenow:

Of the seventy-seven localities where *Homo erectus* fossils have been found, more than half (forty-two) of these sites have also yielded stone tools. At eleven of the *Homo erectus* sites there is evidence of the controlled use of fire. Most significant is that at one of the oldest sites, Swartkrans, South Africa, thought to date between 1.5 and 2 m.y.a., *Homo erectus* fossils have been found in association with both tools and fire. While it is technically impossible to prove that the stone tools and the fire at a given site were made by *Homo erectus* individuals, the sheer number of associations makes it unreasonable to believe otherwise. Three Upper Pleistocene *Homo erectus* sites show evidence of burial, one of a cremation, one of the use of red ochre, and another of the use of bone-chopping tools. We hardly dare ask the archaeological record for more evidence of the true and full humanity of the individuals having a *Homo erectus* morphology. *Lubenow*, 140.

Mankind's Antiquity

Man's presence on the earth long before evolutionists will admit is indicated by the Laetoli footprint trails dated to 3.7 million years ago. Evolutionists attribute these fossil footprints to *A. afarensis*, but that conclusion seems driven more by evolutionary assumptions than by the evidence. As mentioned above, studies have concluded that *A. afarensis* was most likely not fully bipedal in the sense of walking like a human. Yet, the study of the Laetoli footprints by Richard Tuttle of the University of Chicago indicates that they are "indistinguishable from those of habitually barefoot *Homo sapiens*." *Lubenow*, 174. A comparison of the Laetoli footprints with those of Machiguenga Indians of Peru (a habitually barefoot people) revealed "the remarkable humanness of Laetoli hominid feet in all detectable morphological features." *Lubenow*, 174.

Given these findings, Tuttle naturally rejects the claim that the Laetoli footprints were made by *A. afarensis*, but because of his evolutionary convictions, he refuses to attribute them to man. He leaves no doubt as to his reasoning in this regard: "If the G footprints were not known to be so old, we would readily conclude that they were made by a member of our genus, *Homo*." *Lubenow, 175.*

Further evidence of the early presence of man is provided by the Olduvai stone structure dated to about 1.9 million years ago. This is a circular stone structure, fourteen feet in diameter, that was made by the piling up of several hundred lava rocks that had been brought from some miles away. The purpose of this structure is unknown, but members of the Okombambi tribe in Southwest Africa today construct similar rings of stones as the foundation for a wind shelter. *Lubenow, 172-73.*

Recently reported finds by Yuri Mochanov, an archeologist with the Russian Academy of Sciences, indicate that humans lived just below the Arctic Circle at least 500,000 years ago and possibly more than two million years ago. Mochanov has excavated thousands of simple stone tools in northern Siberia which have been dated to at least 500,000 years using a new technique called thermoluminescence. In his opinion, the site is several times older than that. To survive in such a frigid climate, whoever made these tools must have had the ability to develop winter survival strategies, to effectively manage fire, and to make protective clothing such as mitts and boots. *Morell, 611-12.*

"Modern" Mankind's Antiquity

Whether the Laetoli footprints, the Olduvai stone structure, or the Siberian stone tools were made by *Homo erectus* or by more modern appearing humans is unknown. There is evidence that more modern looking forms coexisted with *Homo erectus* from a very early date. As previously mentioned, Lubenow rejects the characterization of Skull 1470, dated to 1.9 million years, as essentially australopithecine, believing instead that it is more modern in appearance than *Homo erectus* specimens. This agrees with Leakey's original appraisal (*Lubenow*, 162) and with the appraisal of William Fix. *Fix*, 135.

The Kanapoi elbow fossil, which dates to 4.5 million years, is remarkably modern in appearance. Multivariate statistical analysis of this fossil, which is in an excellent state of preservation, has shown it to be "indistinguishable from modern *Homo sapiens.*" *Lubenow*, 53. Because of its age, however, evolutionists refuse to assign it to the genus Homo. As William Howells admits:

> The humeral fragment from Kanapoi, with a date of about 4.4 million, could not be distinguished from *Homo sapiens* morphologically or by multivariate analysis by Patterson and myself in 1967 (or by much more searching analysis by others since then). We suggested that it might represent *Australopithecus* because at that time allocation to *Homo* seemed preposterous, *although it would be the correct one without the time element. Lubenow*, 56-57 (emphasis added).

In 1880 Professor Giuseppe Razzagoni, a geologist and teacher at the Technical Institute of Brescia, uncovered a modern skeleton, complete with skull, in Castenedolo, Italy in the Middle Pliocene strata (making it 3-4 million years old). Despite the fact Razzagoni had carefully examined the overlying rocks and determined that they had not been disturbed and the fact the bones of different individuals were mingled and horizontally dispersed over several square meters, his find was ultimately dismissed as a case of intrusive burial! *Cremo*, 422-32, 793. As is apparent from the comment of Sir Arthur Keith, the famed Cambridge

University anatomist, this was done because of a prior commitment to a certain view of evolution:

> As the student of prehistoric man reads and studies the records of the "Castenedolo" find, a feeling of incredulity rises within him. He cannot reject the discovery as false without doing an injury to his sense of truth, and he cannot accept it as a fact without shattering his accepted beliefs. *Pitman*, 247.

In the late 1960's, scientists employed chemical (nitrogen content) and radiometric (carbon 14) tests to assign a young age to the Castenedolo bones, but these tests are by no means conclusive, especially in this case. The rate at which nitrogen in a bone decreases depends on too many local factors to be a reliable chronometer, and the fact the Castenedolo bones were found in clay, a substance known to preserve nitrogen-containing bone proteins, would tend to produce an artificially high nitrogen content. *Cremo*, 432, 755-58.

Interestingly, the chemical studies of the Castenedolo bones also revealed levels of fluorine and uranium that indicated they were older than the age estimate based on their nitrogen content. Rather than conclude that the nitrogen content was artificially high, purely speculative scenarios were invoked to explain away the inconsistent fluorine and uranium readings. *Cremo*, 762-64.

As for the carbon 14 test, bone is not a very suitable material for the test (*Cremo*, 793), and the types of bones dated from the Castenedolo find (ribs and vertebrae) would be highly susceptible to carbon contamination. *Cremo*, 792. Given that standard decontamination procedures were not employed when the Castenedolo bones were tested (*Cremo*, 790-91), there is no reason to accept the carbon 14 date over the exceptionally strong stratigraphic evidence. Indeed, if the bones had been of australopi-thecine morphology, the carbon 14 results would undoubtedly be ignored (as is frequently done).

The handling of the Castenedolo finds is typical of the way other anomalous human skeletal fossils have been treated by the scientific community. The bias against evidence that contradicts the currently accepted scenario of human evolution is so great that some reason is always found for rejecting it. These negative assessments are accepted as gospel truth, and the troublesome discoveries are then purged from the scientific consciousness.

The modern student of archeology will likely never hear of the Buenos Aires skull found in Argentina in 1896 at a level dated to 1-1.5 million years (*Cremo*, 413-18), or of the Foxhall jaw unearthed in England in 1855 at a level dated to 2.5 million years (*Cremo*, 420-21), or of the Savonna skeleton discovered in Italy in the 1850's at a level dated to 3-4 million years (*Cremo*, 433-35), or of the Miramar jaw fragment found in Argentina in 1921 in a formation dated to 2-3 million years. *Cremo*, 438-39. The student will probably not learn the arguments in favor of the 1.15-million-year date for the modern skeleton excavated from upper Bed II of Olduvai Gorge by Professor Hans Reck in 1913 (*Cremo*, 628-49) or the arguments in favor of ancient dates for Leakey's Kanjera skull and Kanam jaw. *Cremo*, 649-61. Such evidence for the great antiquity of modern appearing people has been screened out because it does not fit the controlling paradigm.

Thus, an examination of the fossil record shows clearly that at every turn the proposed evolutionary descent of human beings is a myth. Yet, this myth is so ingrained in the minds of those in the field that they refuse to consider any alternative interpretations of the evidence. The truth is that the fossils do not show an evolutionary sequence from monkey to man. Rather, man suddenly appears in the fossil record and continues to the present, displaying throughout that period of time a range of morphological variation similar to that which exists today.

CONCLUSION

The words of Professor Dean Kenyon provide an apt conclusion to this study. Dr. Kenyon earned a Ph.D. in biophysics from Stanford University and is currently Professor of Biology at San Francisco State University. He was a Post-doctoral Fellow at the University of California at Berkeley and a Visiting Scholar at Oxford University. As an evolutionist, he performed original research on the origin of life, published numerous articles on the subject, and co-authored the book *Biochemical Predestination*. He is now convinced, however, that belief in creation better accords with the evidence:

> It is my conviction that if any professional biologist will take adequate time to examine carefully the assumptions upon which the macroevolutionary doctrine rests, and the observational and laboratory evidence that bears on the problem of origins, he/she will conclude that there are substantial reasons for doubting the truth of this doctrine. Moreover, I believe that a scientifically sound creationist view of origins is not only possible, but is to be preferred over the evolutionary view. . . .
>
> We have seen that evidence often taken to support a naturalistic chemical origin of life, actually, upon close analysis, points in another direction, namely, toward the conclusion that the first life was

created. The data of molecular biology, especially the details of the genetic-coding and protein-synthesizing systems, lend further powerful support to this view. Probability arguments applied to the problem of the origin of genetic information also confirm the creationist view of origins.

Laboratory data and theoretic arguments concerning the origin of the first life lead one to doubt the evolution of subsequent forms of life. The fossil record and other evidence confirm this suspicion. In short, when all the available evidence is carefully assessed in toto, the evolutionary view of origins appears significantly less probable than the creationist view. Bird*, 1:33-34.

BIBLIOGRAPHY

Bartusiak, Marcia, *Through a Universe Darkly* (New York: Harper-Collins, 1993). Bartusiak has an advanced degree in physics and has received the prestigious Science Writing Award from the American Institute of Physics.

Bird, W. R., *The Origin of Species Revisited* (Nashville: Thomas Nelson, 1991; originally published by Philosophical Library in 1987). Bird graduated *summa cum laude* from Vanderbilt University and has a J.D. degree from Yale Law School. He has published articles in numerous law journals and represented the State of Louisiana in the challenge to its "creation statute." Both volumes of this work are extensively documented with references to the pertinent scientific literature.

Brown, Michael H., *The Search for Eve* (New York: Harper & Row, 1990). Brown is an investigative journalist who specializes in science reporting and the author of several books.

Chyba, Christopher, "The Cosmic Origins of Life on Earth," *Astronomy* (Nov. 1992): 28-35. Chyba is a National Research Council Scientist at the NASA Ames Research Center.

Clayton, John, *The Source*, 2d ed. (Mentone, IN: Superior Printing, 1978). Clayton has a M.S. degree in geology and earth science from the University of Notre Dame and is a high school biology teacher in Indiana.

Cremo, Michael A. and Richard L. Thompson, *Forbidden Archeology* (San Diego, CA: Govardhan Hill Publishing, 1993). Thompson has a Ph.D. in mathematics from Cornell and is the author of scientific books and articles on evolutionary biology. Cremo is a research associate specializing in the history and philosophy of science. This work is extensively documented with references to the pertinent scientific literature.

Davies, Paul, *God and the New Physics* (New York: Simon & Schuster, 1983). Davies is an internationally known professor of theoretical physics at University of Newcastle-upon-Tyne, England.

Davis, Percival and Dean H. Kenyon, *Of Pandas and People* (Dallas: Haughton Publishing Co., 1990). Davis has a M.A. degree from Columbia University and is a life science professor at Hillsborough Community College. Kenyon has a Ph.D. in biophysics from Stanford and is Professor of Biology at San Francisco State University. He is the co-author of *Biochemical Predestination* published by McGraw-Hill in 1969. The Academic Editor of *Of Pandas and People* was Charles B. Thaxton who has a Ph.D. in chemistry from Iowa State University and is the co-author of *The Mystery of Life's Origin* published by the Philosophical Library in 1984.

Denton, Michael, *Evolution: A Theory in Crisis* (London: Burnett Books, 1985). Denton has M.D. and Ph.D. degrees from British universities and works as a molecular biology researcher at Prince of Wales Hospital in Australia.

Eichman, Phillip, *Understanding Evolution: A Christian Perspective* (South Bend, IN: John Clayton, 1984). Eichman has a Ph.D. in biology and has taught science, chemistry, and biology on the college level.

Fix, William R., *The Bone Peddlers* (New York: Macmillan Publishing, 1984). Fix has a M.A. degree in behavioral science from Simon Fraser University (Canada) and is the author of several books.

Gange, Robert, *Origins and Destiny* (Dallas: Word, 1986). Gange has a Ph.D. in physics, is a research scientist (over 25 years with David Sarnoff Research Center in Princeton, N.J.), and is a professional engineer. The book is endorsed by Eugene P. Wigner, a recipient of the Nobel Prize for Physics.

Gish, Duane T., *Evolution: The Challenge of the Fossil Record* (San Diego: Creation-Life Publishers, 1985). Gish has a Ph.D. in biochemistry from the University of California at Berkeley and worked for 18 years in biochemical and biomedical research.

————, *Creation Scientists Answer Their Critics* (El Cajon, CA: Institute for Creation Research, 1993).

Godfrey, Laurie R., ed., *Scientists Confront Creationism* (New York: W. W. Norton & Co., 1983). Citations are from the chapter by C. Loring Brace. He is Professor of Anthropology and curator of physical anthropology at the Museum of Anthropology, University of Michigan.

Gould, Stephen J., "The Ediacaran Experiment," *Natural History* (February 1984): 14-23. Gould is a Professor of Geology at Harvard.

Grassé, Pierre-P., *Evolution of Living Organisms* (New York: Academic Press, 1977). Grassé is France's most distinguished zoologist. Dobzhansky has described his knowledge of the living world as "encyclopedic."

Horgan, John, "In the Beginning," *Scientific American* (February 1991): 116-25. Horgan is a senior staff writer for the journal.

_____, "Universal Truths," *Scientific American* (October 1990): 108-17.

Hoyle, Sir Fred and Chandra Wickramasinghe, *Evolution From Space* (New York: Simon & Schuster, 1981). Hoyle is an astronomer and mathematician who taught mostly at Cambridge. He headed the Institute of Theoretical Astronomy at Cambridge until 1972 and is a fellow and former president of the Royal Astronomical Society. Wickramasinghe is an internationally recognized authority on interstellar matter and is the head of the department of applied mathematics and astronomy at University College in Cardiff, Wales.

Kreeft, Peter and Ronald K. Tacelli, *Handbook of Christian Apologetics* (Downers Grove, IL: InterVarsity Press, 1994). Kreeft and Tacelli are both professors of philosophy at Boston College. Kreeft has written many books related to the Christian faith.

Jastrow, Robert, *Until the Sun Dies* (New York: W. W. Norton & Co., 1977). Jastrow has a Ph.D. in theoretical physics from Columbia University and is currently Professor of Earth Sciences at Dartmouth and Director of NASA's Goddard Institute for Space Studies. The author was directed to this work by Dr. Bert Thompson's booklet *The Scientific Case for Creation* (Montgomery, AL: Apologetics Press, n.d.).

Johanson, Donald and James Shreeve, *Lucy's Child* (New York: William Morrow and Company, 1989). Johanson is an internationally recognized paleoanthropologist.

Johnson, Phillip E., "The Extinction of Darwinism," *Atlantic* (Feb. 1992): 103-07. Johnson, a graduate of Harvard and University of Chicago, is a Professor of Law at University of California at Berkeley.

_____, *Darwin on Trial* (Washington, D.C.: Regnery Gateway, 1991).

Kimbel, William H. and others, "The first skull and other new discoveries of *Australopithecus afarensis* at Hadar, Ethiopia," *Nature* 368 (March 31, 1994): 449-51.

Lester, Lane P. and Raymond G. Bohlin, *The Natural Limits to Biological Change*, 2d ed. (Dallas: Probe Books, 1989). Lester has a Ph.D. in genetics from Purdue University and is a Professor of Biology at Liberty University. Bohlin has a M.S. degree in population genetics from North Texas State University and a Ph.D. in molecular biology from the University of Texas.

Lubenow, Marvin L., *Bones of Contention* (Grand Rapids: Baker, 1992). Lubenow is a Professor of Bible and Apologetics at Christian Heritage College. He has studied paleoanthropology for twenty five years. This work is extensively documented with references to the pertinent scientific literature.

Margenau, Henry and Roy Abraham Varghese, eds., *Cosmos, Bios, Theos* (La Salle, IL: Open Court Publishing, 1992). Margenau is currently Emeritus Eugene Higgins Professor of Physics and Natural Philosophy at Yale. He is the author of over 200 research articles and 14 books. Those quoted from this book are internationally known scientists in various fields.

Moreland, J. P., *Scaling the Secular City* (Grand Rapids: Baker, 1987). Moreland has a Ph.D. in philosophy from the University of Southern California and is a Professor of Philosophy at Talbot School of Theology, Biola University.

Morell, Virginia, "Did Early Humans Reach Siberia 500,000 Years Ago?," *Science* 263 (Feb. 4, 1994): 611-12.

Morris, Henry M. and Gary E. Parker, *What is Creation Science* (San Diego: Creation-Life Publishers, 1982). Morris has a Ph.D. in hydraulic engineering from the University of Minnesota. Parker has a M.S. and Ed.D. in biology from Ball State University and is head of the biology department at Christian Heritage College.

Parker, Steve, *The Dawn of Man* (New York: Crescent Books, 1992). Parker studied zoology at Bristol University and then worked at the Natural History Museum, London, arranging exhibits on evolution, paleontology, and human biology. He has edited more than 50 books on life sciences.

Pitman, Michael, *Adam and Evolution* (London: Rider & Co., 1984).Pitman has a B.A. degree in science from Open University (England), a M.A. degree in classics from Oxford, and teaches biology in

Cambridge, England. The introduction is by Dr. Bernard Stone-house, a scientist who has held academic posts at Oxford, Yale, and other prestigious universities.

Pun, Pattle P. T., *Evolution Nature and Scripture in Conflict?* (Grand Rapids: Zondervan, 1982). Pun has a Ph.D. in biology from SUNY and is a Professor of Biology at Wheaton College.

Ross, Hugh, *The Fingerprint of God*, 2d ed. (Orange, CA: Promise Publishing Co., 1991). Ross has a Ph.D. in astronomy from University of Toronto and spent several years doing research as a Post-doctoral Fellow at the California Institute of Technology.

_____, *The Creator and the Cosmos* (Colorado Springs, CO: Nav-Press, 1993).

Sagan, Carl, ed., *Communication With Extraterrestrial Intelligence (CETI)* (Cambridge, MA: MIT Press, 1973). Sagan is a Professor of Astronomy at Cornell. The author was directed to this work by Dr. Bert Thompson's booklet *The Scientific Case for Creation* (Montgomery, AL: Apologetics Press, n.d.).

Schroeder, Gerald L., *Genesis and the Big Bang* (New York: Bantam, 1990). Schroeder has a Ph.D. in physics from M.I.T. and works as an applied physicist.

Shapiro, Robert, *Origins: A Skeptics Guide to the Creation of Life on Earth* (New York: Summit Books, 1986). Shapiro is a Professor of Chemistry at N.Y.U. and an expert on DNA research and on the genetic effect of environmental chemicals. He is the co-author of *Life Beyond Earth*.

Shreeve, "'Lucy,' Crucial Early Human Ancestor, Finally Gets a Head," *Science* 264 (April 1, 1994): 34-35. Shreeve is a science writer.

Sunderland, Luther D., *Darwin's Enigma: Fossils and Other Problems*, 3d ed. (Santee, CA: Master Book Publishers, 1984). Sunderland had a B.S. from Penn. State University and worked as an aerospace engineer with General Electric specializing in automatic flight control systems (died 1987).

Tattersall, Ian, *The Human Odyssey* (New York: Prentice Hall, 1993). Tattersall has a Ph.D. in Geology and Geophysics from Yale and has been curator of the Museum of Natural History in N.Y. since 1971.

Thewissen, J. G. M. and others, "Fossil Evidence for the Origin of Aquatic Locomotion in Archaeocete Whales," *Science* 263 (Jan. 14, 1994): 210-12.

Thomas, J. D., ed., *Evolution and Faith* (Abilene, TX: ACU Press, 1988). The quote is from the chapter by Perry Reeves. He has a Ph.D. in organic chemistry from the University of Texas and has served as Professor of Chemistry at both Southern Methodist University and Abilene Christian University.

Varghese, Roy Abraham, ed., *The Intellectuals Speak Out About God* (Chicago: Regnery Gateway, 1984). Those quoted are Robert Jastrow and Chandra Wickramasinghe. Their credentials appear elsewhere in the bibliography.

Weinberg, Steven, *The First Three Minutes,* updated ed., (New York: Basic Books, 1993). Weinberg received the Nobel Prize for Physics in 1979 and is currently Professor of Science at the University of Texas.

Wesson, Robert, *Beyond Natural Selection* (Cambridge, MA: MIT Press, 1991). Wesson, a transformed political scientist, is Senior Research Fellow at the Hoover Institute in Stanford, California. George Gabor Miklos, head of the Molecular Neurobiology Group and Centre for Molecular Structure and Function at The Australian National University, said of Wesson's book: "without a doubt the best book on evolution that I have read in over a decade of research."

Wright, Richard T., *Biology Through the Eyes of Faith* (San Francisco: Harper & Row, 1989). Wright has a Ph.D. in biology from Harvard and is Professor of Biology at Gordon College. He is the author of numerous articles and is widely sought as a lecturer in biology.

Wysong, Randy L., *The Creation-Evolution Controversy* (Midland, MI: Inquiry Press, 1976). Wysong has a B.S. and D.V.M. from Michigan State University.

INDEX

TO ORDER MORE BOOKS

Copy this form, fill it out, and mail it to: **Ktisis Publishing, 1413 E. Watson Dr., Suite B, Tempe, AZ 85283-3144.** Be sure to include a check or money order payable to Ktisis Publishing in the exact amount of the purchase ($9.95 for each book plus shipping charges and any applicable sales tax—see below.)

Please send me _____ copies of *THE MYTH OF NATURAL ORIGINS*. A check or money order in the amount of $ _____ is enclosed. I understand that if I am not completely satisfied, I may return any books for a full refund of the purchase price (less shipping charges).

Name_____

Company _____

Address_____

City _____State _____ Zip_____

Phone _____Fax _____

Shipping

Book rate: Add $1.80 for the first book and 30 cents for each additional book (surface shipping may take up to four weeks).

Air mail: Add $3.50 for the first book and 60 cents for each additional book.

City and State Sales Tax

Add 6.7% for each book shipped to an Arizona address. No sales tax is required for books shipped to states other than Arizona.

Computed prices for single orders

One book shipped book rate to a non-Arizona address—send $11.75
One book shipped air mail to a non-Arizona address—send $13.45
One book shipped book rate to an Arizona address—send $12.40
One book shipped air mail to an Arizona address—send $14.10

Non-dealer discounts for quantity orders

For orders of 3-9 books, deduct 10% from the cost of books
For orders of 10-19 books, deduct 20% from the cost of books
For orders of 20 or more books, deduct 25% from the cost of books
(To correctly compute the amount to send, these discounts must be taken before adding the shipping charges and sales tax.)